D1051117

THE LAKE
TURNED
UPSIDE
DOWN

SUE DUGAN MOLINE

THE LAKE TURNED UPSIDE DOWN

Copyright ©2020 Sue Dugan Moline

Cover and interior design: TheDuganDesignGroup.com

Cover Montage: Sheri Hooley on Unsplash.com and Samantha Wallace

ISBN 979-8-5722-5394-8

All rights reserved. No part of this publication may be reproduced, stored in a retrieval system, or transmitted in any form or by any means—for example, electronic, photocopy, recording—without the prior written permission of the author. The only exception is brief quotations in printed reviews.

Contact the author at DuganBooks.com

Printed in the United States of America

"I witnessed the Outing tornado damage about a week after the 1969 storm as a 9-year-old youth traveling up north while on vacation with my family. I always remembered that experience. And, in 1984, almost a year after I was hired as a news reporter for the Brainerd Dispatch, I wrote a story on the 15th anniversary of the deadly Outing storm. I remember struggling to find witnesses to interview for the story because most of the survivors were from the Twin Cities.

Fast forward 35 years later, I was in my Dispatch publisher's office when I received a call from Sue (Dugan) Moline, who said she was one of the tornado survivors from a cabin that was swept into Roosevelt Lake during the Outing tornado. I almost dropped the phone. I told her I had waited 35 years for a survivor to tell the story of that tragic day.

With Sue's help, I published two stories about the 50th anniversary of the Outing tornado. Some of those stories were picked up by newspapers across the state who are members of our Forum media network.

I credit Sue for her long hours of dedication in collecting information from survivors and emergency workers about that day in our history. It's a story that people didn't want to talk about for decades, but needed to share as part of the mental healing from one of the most deadly tornadoes in Minnesota history. Her book gives readers a better understanding of how people survived, and learn more about those who lost their lives. It's also a tribute to the emergency workers and local residents who came to the rescue for the small community."

Pete Mohs
Publisher,
Brainerd Dispatch/Echo Journal

Dedication

*I dedicate this book to all of you who
allowed me to interview you, took the time
to call me, emailed me your story or a
story passed on by others, and sent me
your newspapers, pictures, and movies.
This book would not have been possible
without you, and I am very grateful
for each of you. I have been fascinated
by the research and I hope you
enjoy the story.*

Roosevelt Lake

Cass & Crow Wing Counties, Minnesota

Lake Area – 1,585 acres
Deepest Point – 130 feet

Thanks to Carla Cray.

Table of Contents

Introduction

There was a story here—a story that needed to be told and remembered, that wanted to be told. It had been hidden in many places in bits and pieces for almost fifty years.

The story was tucked away in old yellowed newspapers, National Weather Service statistics, home photo albums, and a few old home movies. But mostly it had been stored in people's hearts and memories—hundreds of people, each with a piece of the story burned into their memories.

I had one piece of the story, a memory, but it was just a small part of a very big story; like having one puzzle piece in a 1,000 piece puzzle. I did not even own a newspaper from that time.

Most of us were very young fifty years ago—children or teenagers, maybe young adults, who witnessed an unbelievably tragic event that left its scars on people, towns, lakes, and forests for many years.

Seven identical caskets stood at the front of Bethany Missionary Church on Monday, August 11, 1969. Seven black hearses lined the west side of the church in Bloomington, Minnesota. A thousand people overflowed an auditorium meant to seat eight hundred.

Before the memorial service, our family gathered in the small chapel near the church. My many cousins on my mom's side of the family greeted me timidly, offering shy hugs, but asking no questions. I was still in shock; we all were. The loss of three family members and four friends was emotionally complicated by my own survival. Sadness and euphoric relief are a lot for a teenager to process simultaneously. Why had I lived? Why had they died?

I attended the funeral in the light blue dress I had worn at my high school graduation just two months earlier. I limped into the church with the long procession of family members of the dead; my feet still hurting from multiple nail punctures and my face showing signs of a black eye.

I usually cry at funerals. I would have grieved better if it had been only my sister Becky's funeral, or my Grandma Dugan's, or my cousin Sharon's. I would have processed it much more personally, remembered them individually, missed them terribly, and sobbed openly.

Because the funeral was for seven people, very little was said about each of the victims personally. The pastor read the obituaries that appeared in the paper. There simply wasn't time to remember them all as separate individuals. I understood why, but this significant omission kept many of us from processing and grieving appropriately for many years.

The funeral message was titled "From Tragedy to Triumph," which the local newspaper later printed word-for-word. I understood the "tragedy" part. I had survived an unthinkable tragedy and lost family members. The "triumph" part was a lot harder to comprehend. Our lives had been forever changed.

⌣

We had enjoyed the first three days of a planned two-week vacation at Roosevelt Lake, a family reunion with many of my Dugan cousins, aunts, and uncles. Two other Bethany families were vacationing with us, the Brokkes and the Carlsons. In all, twenty-eight of us occupied four little three-bedroom cabins. Twenty-two were on the property when the tornado hit while six had left just minutes before to run errands in a nearby town. Seven would be killed.

For many years afterward, I wondered why none of us ever compared our individual stories of the 1969 tornado. I had a one-minute memory of my experience that played over and over in my head, which I shared with anyone who asked, but we didn't know each other's stories. We didn't know what we didn't know.

⌣

In the late '90s, about thirty years after the tornado and now a married adult with four kids of my own, I visited my aging parents at their Bethany apartment. Our family rarely talked about the tornado, except to simply refer to it as "the tornado." I mentioned to both of them my desire to interview all the survivors, hear their stories, and see what they remembered.

My dad looked me in the eye and said, "*Why* would you want to do that?"

It wasn't a question so much as an admonishment. The memories were painful, and he didn't want them brought up again. He didn't want to go there, so I dropped the idea.

I finally decided to search the internet for any information about the tornado that I could find. To my amazement, there was much to be discovered! Through the National Weather Service

website, I learned that it had been an F4 tornado with winds ranging from 207-260 miles per hour. I thought to myself, *And fifteen
of us made it through! How? And why?*

Suddenly our survival seemed almost miraculous.

I could no longer contain my curiosity. I wanted to hear everyone's stories. I had lived with my brief memory for long enough.

A few years later, in 2012, we had a Dugan family reunion
at the big red barn at Bethany International (formerly Bethany
Fellowship), the property where I grew up. It was a well-planned
event called the Dugan County Fair, which included matching
t-shirts, games for the kids, tables of memorabilia, storytelling by
Uncle Dick, and family history. And, of course, we enjoyed a great
picnic too. Relatives from across the country and even around the
world came to catch up with other Dugans. My cousin Don, orig-
inally from southern California, who had survived the tornado as
a fourteen-year-old, now lived in Oregon and needed to be picked
up from the airport. I had only seen Don two or three times in the
previous forty-three years, so I hardly knew him anymore. He had
four children and looked like a rugged Oregonian with longer hair
and a full beard. I wasn't sure what to say or how we would interact
after not seeing one another for so many years.

I picked Don up at the Minneapolis-St. Paul airport and was
driving down Normandale Boulevard when I brought up the tornado. It was one of the few memories we shared.

"Do you ever think about the tornado?" I asked. "What do
you remember?"

Without knowing it I had turned on a faucet. The story just
poured out of him! He had survived that traumatic event at age
fourteen, but his family had returned home to California and
never talked about it. He had kept his memories locked up for

forty-three years. He told me he had finally written his story down about three years previously and would email it to me. By the time we arrived at our destination, Don was sobbing as he got out of my car. I had uncovered some painful memories that really needed to be unearthed and discussed.

Five years later in 2017, I attended another family reunion with my mom's side of the family. Some of my younger cousins started asking me about the tornado. They had all attended the funeral as children, but their parents had told them not to ask any questions, so they knew very little of the story.

In the spring of 2018, I heard that Dale Carlson, another tornado survivor who now lived in Tennessee, was traveling to Minnesota to visit his dad that July. I had not seen or talked to him for probably forty-five years, so I set up a meeting with my aunt, Diane (Dugan) Dahlen, my uncle, Terry Dugan, Dale Carlson, and myself. We had all survived the tornado together as teenagers. Dale came prepared with newspaper copies and an amazing memory for details. He shared things I had never heard before, like seeing the refrigerator in our cabin fly over his head as our cabin started moving, and finding dead fish lying on the road up the hill, *100 feet from the lake*. I recorded much of our conversation and the four of us talked for hours.

That had me hooked—I had to know more. It was then that I decided to gather the stories of everyone who was still alive. I wasn't going to wait until we lost any more survivors or even our own memories. It was time to start asking questions.

My research began in earnest in 2018, roughly one year before the fiftieth anniversary of the Outing tornado. Each story I heard, each person I talked to, and each email I received filled in another missing piece of a very complicated puzzle.

Since then, I have recorded most of the conversations with the survivors from the Bethany Fellowship cabins—my brothers Lon and Jon Dugan, my aunt, Barb Dugan and her sons Ron and Don, my aunt, Priscilla Dugan and her children Shane and Sheila, my Aunt Diane, and my Uncle Terry, Cathy Brokke and her son Dan Brokke, Harold Carlson and his sons Dale and Darrell. (Harold Carlson passed away on December 31, 2019, at age ninety-eight, eight months after I interviewed him.) Five memories are gone forever: my dad Toby, my mom Vonnie, Uncle Kenny, Uncle Dick, and Harold Brokke.

In June of 2019, after placing ads in northern Minnesota papers looking for information, my phone started ringing and my email box started filling up. I spent hours on the phone and took copious notes from survivors and eyewitnesses. I talked to the only-surviving Cass County Sheriff, the Cass County historical society, the Minnesota Department of Natural Resources (who sent me aerial pictures of the affected area), and the National Weather Service. I interviewed Bill Matthies, the diver who found the last two bodies in the lake two days after the tornado.

What you are about to read has been made possible by well over 100 eyewitness reports and is the first comprehensive narrative of what happened in Outing that day.

Gathering these eyewitness accounts has made me realize how much more I needed to heal from this experience, even all these years later. We all held onto the sadness and pain with our silence. I suppose we didn't know how to begin the conversation.

This story is more than fifty years in the making and one that I never thought I'd tell, but as painful as it has been to relive this event, it would be more tragic to forget it entirely. After being married forty-seven years to my husband Scott, my high school sweetheart, with four grown daughters and thirteen grandchildren, I realized I must not assume these memories will be passed on. I simply don't want them forgotten.

I am sixty-seven years old now, but this story begins when I was seventeen.

I Remember...

*I don't remember seeing the tornado or
even hearing it coming.*

*I remember being in the cabin when several other family members and friends raced
down the hill and into the cabin with me.*

*I remember the wind picking up and
watching as it blew a boat through the air
past our cabin with 17 of us
crammed inside.*

*I remember the cabin moving beneath me
and feeling like a rug had been pulled out
from under me.*

*I remember hitting the water and realizing I was in the lake, being tossed by huge
waves. When I finally surfaced, I did not
see even one other living person.*

I remember screaming, "God save us!"

*I remember finally seeing other people start
to pop up in the lake; I remember climbing
out; I remember heading to the hospital.*

But that's all I remember.

CHAPTER ONE

Gone Fishing

We actually thought that our tornado story would not be believed and we were more worried that our parents would smell beer on our breath!
—PATRICK COUGHLIN

The day the lake turned upside down began like any other for the Coughlin boys. It was a Wednesday in August 1969, and a hot one for north-central Minnesota. Although the parents of seventeen-year-old Pat and eighteen-year-old George operated Kilworry Resort on Upper Whitefish Lake, a large lake on a chain of fourteen, the boys had a special fishing hole on Stewart Lake for catching walleye seven miles north of the resort. The Ramerth brothers, two friends from Minneapolis, joined Pat and George on their fishing expedition.

Stewart Lake had no road access—the isolation of the mile-long lake was part of the adventure. Early that morning, the four teens packed up their fishing gear, lunches, and two little boat motors and headed north to a local man's home, who had access to the lake. Larry Glover had a homemade "swamp buggy" to get them there, and his $20 fee was well worth it.

It took about an hour for Larry to transport the boys and their gear the two miles through the swamp and mud to Stewart Lake, where a couple of old, leaky wooden boats waited for them. They planned to fish all day, and as usual, Larry would pick them up in the late afternoon or early evening, in time to return home before dark.

The wind's direction changed frequently that day, fronts whipping around them from all directions. Toward the middle of the afternoon, the four boys noticed a rotating cloud approaching from the west toward the town of Backus. Around the same time, another cloud system sped in their direction from the southeast.

They discussed the weather, certain the clouds could produce a tornado. But where could they go? The boats sat near the middle of the lake and there was no shelter available anywhere. With no way to escape the storm or communicate with their parents back at the resort, they pulled into shore for a while and then decided to just keep fishing. The walleye fishing was amazing that day, and by the time the funnel appeared, they were throwing fish back to avoid exceeding their legal limit.

The wind picked up quickly, darkness extending across the sky as the two storm systems collided over the mile-long lake. Suddenly, Pat saw two waterspouts form at the east end of the lake, and almost immediately a slender gray funnel emerged from the clouds and moved northeast. By now it was late afternoon, sometime after 4:30 p.m.

Larry and his swamp buggy picked up the group earlier than usual that evening after a worried phone call from the Coughlin boys' mother. The boys returned to the resort with their walleye, quite sure that no one would believe their tornado story. They were actually more concerned that their parents would smell beer on their breath. Instead, they returned to very worried parents and a heroes' welcome from the entire resort of fourteen cabins, approximately sixty people.

Little did they know that the tornado, which formed over Stewart Lake, had picked up speed and size as it raced northeast, blowing through thousands of acres of forest and across smaller lakes, destroying everything in its path.

Over a period of seven and a half hours, two cyclic super cells spawned thirteen tornadoes across central and northern Minnesota, ranging from F0 all the way to F4. The boys had seen just the beginnings of the F4 tornado, which stayed on the ground for thirty-eight miles, the width spanning over a mile and a half. By the time it reached Roosevelt Lake in Outing, the storm had become very deadly.

August 6, 1969, became the fifth deadliest day in Minnesota tornado history, killing a total of fifteen people statewide in what the National Weather Service later called the *Northwoods Tornado Outbreak*. Eleven of those deaths occurred on the east and west shores of Roosevelt Lake at 4:55 p.m. in the tiny town of Outing with a twelfth death a few miles northeast on Reservoir Lake. There had been no warnings.

Dozens of cabins, resorts, and vacation homes sat in the path of the F4 tornado as it blew through the Outing area, affecting countless lives for decades to come. More unbelievable than the tragedy of those who died is the miracle that anyone survived at all.

CHAPTER TWO

The Summer of '69

The sun shone, the water gleamed clear as crystal, and America had just landed on the moon. It was promising to be a perfect summer vacation.

The summer of 1969 was a historic one in America. Chappaquiddick occurred on July 18–19 with the scandal involving Senator Ted Kennedy following. On July 20, a successful Apollo 11 spaceflight landed the first men on the moon. On August 9–10, Charles Manson and his family of cult members murdered six people in California. And on August 15–17, the Woodstock Rock Festival was held at a farm near Woodstock, New York, attracting an audience of more than 400,000 with its promise of three days of peace and music. It was a summer packed with major news events.

But the summer of 1969 is memorable to me for other

reasons, the first one being that it was the year I graduated from high school. The more momentous and life-altering reason is the topic of this book.

That May, more than six hundred high school seniors gathered for our final assembly at Lincoln High School in Bloomington, Minnesota. My uncle, Terry Dugan, was just ten days older than me and also in my graduating class. We had explained many times that we weren't brother and sister, or cousins, but uncle and niece. Terry was my dad's brother, younger by twenty-four years. My grandparents had seven children. My dad, Toby, was the oldest and Terry was the youngest. We were both seventeen when we graduated.

I sat near the back of the large auditorium with about 640 other graduating seniors. The assembly covered final graduation details, none of which I paid much attention to, but the speaker also gave a warning in the form of a statistic. He said that in a class our size, a percentage of us would be dead by our ten-year reunion. I don't remember the exact statistic but I do know that it was alarming enough to get my attention. I looked around the auditorium and felt a little smug. I was graduating in the top 10 percent of my class, didn't drink and drive, didn't do drugs, and certainly wasn't going to Vietnam. It definitely wasn't going to be me.

I grew up at Bethany Fellowship in Bloomington, Minnesota, a unique community founded in the 1940s by five Lutheran families with a vision for training, sending, and supporting missionaries. A missionary training center was started as well as industries to support the work. Students and staff members all lived on campus and worked together building Bethany pop-up campers and lefse grills, and publishing Christian books. Bethany Missionary Church, located on the campus, became a thriving church that served the staff and students as well as outside community members.

The summer of '69, the Dugans planned a two-week vacation with extended family at the Bethany Cabins. Part of the fun of every vacation was finally living in a normal house. At Bethany, we lived on the second floor of a dormitory called the Long House. The long hallway on the second floor had a door in the middle that split the living quarters in half. My family occupied the north side, which consisted of seven bedrooms, two bathrooms, and a living room at the end. We did not have a kitchen since we ate communally with the other Bethany families and students in a large campus cafeteria a short walk from the Long House. After living most of our lives in a campus dormitory, vacationing in a cabin with our own kitchen and having our mom cook for us made us feel more like an average family.

My grandma, Edith Dugan, the family matriarch, and her youngest children, twenty-year-old Diane and seventeen-year-old Terry, had moved into our building at Bethany after my grandfather unexpectedly passed away five years earlier. We lived together like one big family. Diane and Terry felt more like siblings to me than an aunt and uncle, and I was closer to them than my own brothers, who were five and nine years younger. Our families had little money, so Diane and I took advantage of being the same size by sharing clothes—it doubled our small school wardrobes.

Because Bethany staff members took only a small monthly allowance it was always a challenge to plan an affordable family vacation. I remember quite a few camping trips in my early years using one of the Bethany pop-up campers.

In 1963, Andrew F. Johnson, father of Morry Johnson a founding member of Bethany Fellowship, turned over ownership of his lakeside property and his hand-built two-bedroom cabin on Roosevelt Lake near the little township of Outing, to the staff of Bethany Fellowship. The population of Outing was about 235 in 1969. Like all northern Minnesota lake towns, the population grew drastically in the summer when resorts opened and cabin owners spent time up north. The Outing area was surrounded by quite a few lakes such as Washburn, Lawrence, and Leavitt, as well as many smaller ones, but the largest lake by far was Roosevelt Lake.

Roosevelt was a deep clear lake, about 129 feet deep on the south end and 70 feet deep on the north end. It had just over eighteen miles of shoreline and stretched in a slightly south-west-to-northeast direction in two sections—a north section and south section connected by a channel, or the narrows. Downtown Outing was located just east of the narrows, a cluster of businesses and a post office that served the area. Highway 6 crossed over the narrows via a bridge from the east side of the lake to the west side and continued on north to Remer.

Work soon began on the newly-owned Bethany property, putting up three new cabins and remodeling the original, naming them in typical Bethany fashion: Cabins 1, 2, 3, and 4. Only the original cabin, Cabin 1, had a basement—the others did not. Cabins 1 and 2 were located on the top of a steep hill near the gravel road that rimmed the northeast side of the lake, at least 40 feet above lake level. Cabins 3 and 4 sat at the bottom of the steep curved driveway on a small peninsula at lake level, close to the shoreline and facing roughly north.

Since Bethany Fellowship owned the cabins and my parents were Bethany staff members, they reserved one for our family vacation every summer. On Sunday, August 3, my dad and mom, Toby and Vonnie, my nineteen-year-old sister Becky, brothers twelve-year-old Lon and nine-year-old Jon, and I drove the three hours from Bloomington to Outing on the now very familiar route. We also towed a Bethany pop-up camper for overflow sleeping and set it up between the two cabins by the lake. My sister Becky had been born with a mental handicap, so although she was older than me by seventeen months, I had taken on the role of oldest child from a very young age. We shared one of the three small bedrooms.

In Cabin 1 at the top of the hill were the Carlsons—Harold and Evy, with their two youngest sons, nineteen-year-old Darrell and seventeen-year-old Dale. Joining them were Evy's parents, the Reverend Arthur and Minnie Olson, who came to the cabins to stay with the Carlsons and celebrate Minnie's eightieth birthday on August 7. They had returned to the United States a few years previously after serving forty-nine years as Lutheran missionaries in China.

Arthur told incredible stories of working in famine re-lief during the 1920s, housing hundreds of refugees during the murderous rampage of Mao Zedong, countless encounters with the military, and the couple's time in a Japanese concentration camp. Arthur had miraculously survived a church bombing, two plane crashes, and the 1964 Great Alaskan Earthquake while on a preaching trip. After living half a century surrounded by life-or-death situations, returning to the U. S. and retiring near their children was very special. They really looked forward to this week at the lake with their daughter's family and celebrating Minnie's birthday.

It was also a busy summer of weddings for the Carlson family. Their only daughter, Darlene, had been married on June 20 with her Grandpa Olson officiating. Their oldest sons, twins David and Daniel, were going to be married on September 4 (both brides were named Nancy) in a double wedding. It promised to be a great summer of celebrations.

My grandma Edith Dugan, Terry and Diane, and their older brother Kenny and his family were staying in Cabin 2 at the top of the steep hill overlooking the lake. My Uncle Kenny and Aunt Barb had arrived from southern California with their two sons, seventeen-year-old Ron and fourteen-year-old Don. Kenny was the sales manager at a 3M office in North Hollywood and it was really special to return to Minnesota to spend a couple of weeks with his mom and siblings.

We were staying in Cabin 3, down by the lake. With us were my Uncle Dick and Aunt Priscilla Dugan, who came from South Dakota with their children, nine-year-old Sheila, six-year-old Shane, and five-year-old Sharon, with a fourth child soon on the way. At that time, Dick was pastor of a large church in Huron, South Dakota.

Dugans dominated the vacation site and we were not a quiet bunch. Late-night get-togethers with storytelling, jokes, and reminiscing were the norm when the family got together.

Fellow staff members and close friends, Harold (our pastor) and Cathy Brokke, an RN and talented organist, and their sons seventeen-year-old Dan and thirteen-year-old Paul were in Cabin 4 down on the lakeshore. Harold Brokke was recovering from a very recent cornea transplant, but the doctor cleared him to go on vacation provided that he stay away from high winds and bumpy roads.

Altogether, twenty-eight of us traveled north for a long-awaited vacation at the lake. We arrived on Sunday, August 3, and planned to stay for two weeks. The three newer cabins were very well-built three-bedroom cabins, and each had a big picture window facing the lake. They also each had a wood-burning stove for winter use. They had been constructed on cement block footings rather than on a cement slab, so the cabins sat a foot or more off the ground. This became a very important detail.

The four cabins also shared a speedboat, a couple of small fishing boats, a pontoon, a canoe, and water skis—everything we needed for a very enjoyable vacation.

My goal for the vacation as a somewhat adventurous seventeen-year-old was to learn how to slalom water ski and I hoped to have that mastered by the end of the two-week vacation. We fished, we swam, we water skied, and the many kids and teens jumped into the lake from a rope swing hanging from a large oak tree about 50 feet down the shoreline from Cabin 3. Diane and I took my sister, Becky, out in the canoe a few times. Becky couldn't paddle herself, but she'd sit in the middle and we'd paddle around the bay. On Tuesday night, the evening before the storm, the Brokkes invited me to their cabin to play a board game. Cathy kindly told me how nice it was to have a girl around since she only had boys.

Although the mosquitoes seemed the size of small birds and seemingly could empty the blood from your body overnight, it was a wonderful place. We could catch all the sunfish, bass, and northern pike we wanted. The sun shone, the water gleamed clear as crystal, and America had just landed on the moon. It was promising to be a perfect summer vacation.

CHAPTER THREE

A Strange Dream

"It's just a scary dream," my mom assured him in her practical, matter-of-fact manner. "Don't worry about it."

Edith and Diane Dugan shared a bedroom in Cabin 2 on the top of the hill. Edith woke Diane up in the middle of the night early Wednesday. A bear stood outside the cabin window and they watched it for a while. Diane wasn't sure what had awakened her mom—perhaps the noise of the bear or perhaps she just couldn't sleep.

Edith had been sick with a cold the week prior to the vacation, spending a few days in bed. Diane couldn't help but notice a deep, quiet sadness in her mother. When the two of them went to the store to buy Diane a swimming suit for the vacation, Edith sat in the fitting room quietly, a look of complete desolation on her face. It had been five years since her husband had died and she was still laden with grief. At barely twenty years of age, Diane was grieved to see her sadness but just didn't have the words to address it. Edith was her mom, and moms were supposed to be okay.

Their lives had turned upside down after Diane's dad, my grandpa, died suddenly in 1964, and the family had to adjust to a new and unusual way of living. Shortly after his death, Edith and her three children, Pat, Diane, and Terry moved to the Bethany campus to become a part of the community. Edith and Diane roomed together those five years. It was a very small space, but my family lived across the hall, and Diane thought it was kind of fun to be around family all the time. Her dad's unexpected passing made her hesitant to go places, especially overnight, because she thought something might happen in her absence. A fear of her mother dying plagued Diane. Her mom clearly missed Diane's dad, Bernard. Diane's older brother, Pat, would come home from work and find Edith sitting in her pink chair, eyes red from weeping. But nothing was ever said.

The week before the vacation, Bethany Fellowship held its annual summer missions conference. Diane stayed after one of the services to talk with Cathy Brokke about her fears. The two prayed together, and Diane surrendered her mother into God's care.

↩

On Wednesday morning, August 6, my nine-year-old brother, Jon, woke up from a disturbing dream of our sister Becky's death. He told our mom that morning, pulling on her sleeve as she made breakfast.

"Mom, I dreamed that Becky died! Her body was near some trees and covered by a blanket. You were standing over her," he said, brown eyes wide.

"It's just a scary dream," my mom assured him in her practical, matter-of-fact manner. "Don't worry about it."

Wednesday had been a fun day of playing ball, fishing, waterskiing, and swimming. Cathy Brokke was making egg rolls for supper and her two boys, Paul and Dan, teamed up against Dick and Terry in Wiffle ball until around 4:00 p.m.

The competitive Brokke boys found their match in Dick and Terry, who played with just as much fervor. The three of them joked about Paul looking like a stick standing on the mound, since he was rather skinny. The thirteen-year-old redhead didn't seem to mind—he loved Wiffle ball too much to care and they were winning this game. Dale Carlson came down the hill looking for some fishing buddies for that evening. He already had the fishing boat on a trailer and ready to go up at the top of the hill.

My dad and my twelve-year-old brother Lon set about transforming one of the rowboats into a sailboat.

At some point during the day, someone mentioned a tornado watch out for the area. Diane wasn't fazed. Her dad had been leery of storms, high winds especially, but this was Minnesota—tornado warnings went out all the time. She didn't give it a second thought.

After asking their parents, nine-year-olds Sheila and Jon walked a mile to the bait shop in town to buy candy with their vacation allowance. The two cousins liked to hang around each other whenever their families got together. On the way, they crossed the bridge that sat over the channel from Roosevelt Lake to the adjacent Lawrence Lake, just east of the tiny town of Outing.

"What would you do if there were a tornado?" Sheila asked her cousin. They had heard whispers of tornadoes earlier that day.

"I know you have to get down low, so maybe get in the ditch or something?"

"Like that one down there?" She pointed a few yards away.

"Sure, maybe."

They bought their candy and started to walk back to the cabins. Jon held his pixie sticks gallantly, the scary dream from the night before long forgotten.

Dick and Priscilla's family were sharing our cabin at the bottom of the hill, and at some point in the early afternoon, I found myself in the living room. Priscilla, who was seven months pregnant, sat in a comfortable chair on the other side of the room with rollers in her hair. Somewhere a radio played in the background and the word *tornado* came up in the broadcast as part of a storm watch. Tornadoes had already passed through northern Minnesota earlier that day, the first touching down in Beltrami County near Bemidji at 1:15 p.m.

"A tornado would never hit us," I said confidently to my aunt, "We're in a low-lying area. It would jump right over the lake." I gave it no more thought. We were used to several tornado warnings each summer in Minnesota, always being told to go to the basement or a low-lying area. But at home in Bloomington, those warnings were always announced with a civil defense siren also.

During the late afternoon, the air became very still, muggy, and oppressively hot. We tried to get news on the radio, but the static on the transistor made it impossible to hear weather reports. Then the winds picked up.

CHAPTER FOUR

Without Warning

The lake turned green!
~JOE ARMSTRONG, AGE 6

Because of the increasing wind and overcast sky, everyone got out of the lake and headed to their cabins. My dad decided this would be an opportune time to make a run to Emily, the town seven miles south, to buy parts at the hardware store for his makeshift sailboat. He and my brother, Lon, took off in the car and met Jon and Sheila on the gravel road walking home. The kids wanted to go back to the cabins and play, but my dad insisted they ride with him to the hardware store. It had started to drizzle, and Sheila didn't want to get wet, so they agreed.

Harold Carlson and his older son, Darrell, also departed for Emily to bring Arthur Olson's old car to a garage. It had broken down on the drive north and the retired missionary was scheduled to preach in a nearby town that coming Sunday. Harold said goodbye to his wife, Evy, and planned to be back by dinnertime.

In total, six people from the Bethany Cabins left the premises at about 4:45 p.m.

My dad and Lon anticipated that the strong wind would improve their sailing efforts. Before they had driven very far from Outing to pick up the parts, my dad looked in the rearview mirror.

"Boy, that is a big, black cloud," he remarked. They continued on their trip.

A few minutes before 5:00 p.m., the people in Edith Dugan's cabin on the hill noticed thick black clouds moving across the lake from the southwest. Intrigued, Diane walked out on the deck to get a better look.

"It looks like a tornado, but there's no funnel," Diane's older brother, Dick, mused, standing on the front porch.

The dark, swirling winds quickly escalated in moments, and panic set in. They needed to get to lower ground *now*! Everyone in the cabin started running down the steep hill.

"Run, run, run!" someone screamed. Six-year-old Shane, barefoot, struggled painfully to get down the rough driveway. He got about halfway when his cousin, Ron, bolted out of our cabin, ran up the driveway, quickly scooped him up, and carried him back to safety.

Diane realized that everyone else was heading down the hill and quickly joined them. Her mom, moving slower than everyone else, lagged behind. Diane waited for her to catch up and they moved as quickly as they could into the cabin.

Dick yelled on his way down the hill, "It's a tornado! We could see its shape from up top!"

Diane and my grandma entered the cabin nearest to the driveway with the others. Fifteen people now gathered inside.

Priscilla told Shane and five-year-old Sharon to get under the beds in the back bedroom, which were bolted to the floor. Diane stood in the living room and looked out the window. The wind bent the small trees in front of the cabin parallel to the ground.

In the other lower cabin, Harold Brokke called his wife, Cathy, over to the window. The wind roared louder and louder. The patch over Harold's eye from his recent cornea transplant considerably obscured his vision, but he thought he saw something strange across the lake. The couple thought it could be a tornado, but they didn't see a funnel, only a wall of dark, massive, moving clouds. Since there was no basement or storm shelter, they and their sons, Paul and Dan, ran next door to the Dugan cabin and discovered their friends from the other cabin already gathered there.

"A tornado's coming!" Dan exclaimed, rushing into the cabin. Cathy and Paul followed closely behind him.

Harold Brokke didn't enter the cabin, but rather grabbed onto a tree right outside. Dan saw his dad hanging on as the tree began to crack. The seventeen-year-old dashed out the cabin's side door and threw himself against his father, pushing them both to the ground.

By this time, seventeen people occupied our cabin. About half huddled in the back bedroom, trying to get as far away from the window as possible. The rest of us stood frozen in the living room and kitchen, gaping out the windows toward the lake. I saw a rowboat fly past the window as smoothly as if it were in water.

This is not looking good, I thought.

Then suddenly the cabin jerked and began to move as though a rug was pulled out from beneath us. The wind screamed like a freight train; the floor screeched like a million hammers pulling nails out of wood. The entire cabin, with all of us inside, flew through the air and was slammed into the water. Terry's mind flashed to *The Wizard of Oz*. The refrigerator flew over Dale's head. Don felt his back collide with the wood stove. Cathy tucked her head. Diane felt as though she was being pitched down a churning river. Priscilla felt a splash of water on her face. *Oh God, not the lake. God, protect my babies,* was all she could think before crashing into the water.

I don't remember the sound of the wind, but I remember the fear. Everything happened too quickly for me to react. All I remember is the Brokkes entering the cabin and then the sudden moving of the house. The fear was paralyzing—all those Minnesota tornado warnings and now I was in one!

The tornado swept through the property in just over a minute. It flung the cabin and everyone in it into a 40-foot wall of water pushed up by 200 plus mile-an-hour spinning winds. Amazingly, the cabin stayed intact until we hit the lake.

CHAPTER 5

A Thousand Ways to Die

*It was like being caught in a giant whirlpool. It had
tremendous driving force. It forced the water right into
my mouth and pressed the flesh right against my bones.*
— Ken Dugan

All the survivors recount the same basic memories: tumbling
helplessly in the lake, getting a gulp of air, and being dragged
underwater again with no idea of what would become of them.

I spun out of control under the water, eyes closed. Two or
three times I got a quick breath of air before being pulled under
water again. My mind flickered back to the speech at my high
school senior assembly. *I'm being carried by a tornado and I am
going to die. Terry and I will be one of those statistics.*

～

The dark water tossed fourteen-year-old Don Dugan around as

he gasped for air. When he surfaced, he caught sight of Becky ten feet away, futilely trying to grasp onto anything to stay afloat. Don was powerless to do anything to help her. The water sucked him under again before he could get another breath, and he held it for as long as he could. Soon his body demanded oxygen and he instinctively inhaled—air filled his lungs! Whether it was from an air pocket or some miracle, Don had no clue.

"I opened my eyes once under the water and saw all the debris floating above me: there were crates and boards and mattresses. I went up and the storm was over."

Don surfaced 30 yards offshore under a sunny sky. A short distance away, he spotted his mom struggling in the water to hold onto some wreckage. Barb had been dragged so deeply into the lake that it was impossible to know which way was up. She saw a spot of light and decided to scissors kick toward it. After finally surfacing, she barely had enough energy to stay afloat.

"Hang on, Mom!" he called, swimming in her direction. Barb later told Don that she was just about to give up paddling when she heard his voice.

Ron, age seventeen, was wearing a white t-shirt and 501 Levi jeans that day, making it hard to swim. When he surfaced in the lake, he was totally disoriented, wondering if he was still even in the same lake! He recognized nothing. He swam toward the nearest shoreline and then saw something familiar. He recognized the huge roots of the oak tree the rope swing had been hanging from. The entire tree was gone, but the twisted roots that were used for climbing out of the water after dropping into the lake still remained. Finally, he knew where he was.

The wind pulled Kenny Dugan deep underwater. He told a newspaper reporter: "It was like being caught in a giant whirlpool. It had tremendous driving force. It forced the water right into my mouth and pressed the flesh right against my bones." He had to swim a significant distance to get to the surface only to discover that he had been deposited toward the middle of the lake, a few hundred feet from shore. His son, Ron, already onshore, watched him slowly crawl toward land. When he finally made it, the 41-year-old was exhausted, gasping for air before collapsing on some branches. His wife, Barb, feared that he would have a heart attack. Ken unzipped the light jacket he was wearing. The inside was completely dry.

⌒

Blasts of dirt pummeled Dan and Harold Brokke as they clung to each other on the ground outside the cabin. A small tree fell on their backs—Dan reached over to lift it and the wind threw his arm back behind him as it pulled the tree away. After a minute of unbearable roaring, the wind stopped.

Muddy, wind-blown, and disoriented, Harold and Dan rose to their feet and stared at the destruction, unable to comprehend what they saw.

Other than a few small saplings, all the trees had been up-rooted and pushed flat against the ground. The heavily wooded hillside lay completely bare. The boats and docks were gone; the cars were gone; the only thing left of the two lower cabins was their imprints in black patches of dirt. Cathy and Paul were nowhere to be seen. Dan had the sinking feeling that he would never see Paul alive again. His brother was afraid of water and would have panicked. As for his mom—well, Dan hoped desperately that she would make it.

Harold finally spoke. "There was something inside that just

wouldn't let me go in that cabin. I couldn't go in there."

"Everything is gone. There's nothing left," Dan whispered numbly.

"Do you see your mom?" Harold asked.

"I don't see anybody," Dan replied. Terrified, he cried out for Jesus.

Dan looked at his father and back at the destruction. A quiet peace washed over him.

The last of the seven-foot waves in the narrow lake crashed into the shore. Harold asked again, "Do you see your mom or Paul?" Dan did not.

Then in the next few moments, Dan saw heads bob up in the water. He was at first afraid to wade into the rough, debris-strewn waters, but people began to yell for help. Then he saw his mom about 200 feet from shore. He plunged into the lake and swam to her. She had dog-paddled herself to the surface and found a piece of floating wood to cling to. The surface of the lake was covered with complete sides of cabins and a massive amount of debris. Blood streamed from an eight-inch gash in Cathy's scalp.

Dan saw the floor of a cabin floating nearby. "Mom, can you get up here?"

"I can't," she said, dazed from multiple blows to the head. Dan was able to partially lift her onto the cabin floor and climbed on himself.

"Have you seen Paul?" Cathy asked through pained delirium. Dan told her that he had not. He tried to think of a way to get people onshore and attempted to flip a capsized boat over. That's when he saw a gray sweatshirt floating nearby. Becky was lying face down in the water.

Dan made sure that Cathy had a solid hold onto the cabin

floor and slid back into the water to grab Becky. He turned her over and pulled the three of them to shore. Cathy saw her clutch purse with her cosmetics floating by and plucked it out of the water as they rode the waves.

$\backsim$

Diane's limbs flew around helplessly in the pitch-black water. She thought, *This is it. I better get my life squared with God*, and then, *Oh, I guess I'm okay with Him*. The next thought was, *They will find my body downstream tomorrow*.

She surfaced in the middle of debris with a utility cable tight around her neck. She yanked it off and looked around.

Where am I? The landscape had changed so drastically it was impossible to tell.

Then Diane saw Dan Brokke, who pulled her out of the water. In shock, she walked a little distance up the hill. She didn't know what to do with herself, so stood helplessly with her back to the lake. She had heard someone say, "Here's the body of an older woman." Instinctively, she knew it was her mother and could not bear such a sight.

$\backsim$

When he surfaced, Terry spotted his nephew Shane clutching a piece of debris ten feet away. Something had deeply gashed his forehead above his right eyebrow and his head had swollen to twice its size. Bruises covered his body, but Shane's eyes were wide open.

"Hang on, Shane!" Terry called, grabbing onto the six-year-old. They had been swept out about 300 feet north from where the cabins used to stand, now about 50 feet away from the east shoreline.

"You'll be okay, just hang on. Hang on!"

Terry saw Dale Carlson a short distance away. Dale had to propel himself up 20 feet through the water to get to the surface. The three boys hung on to anything they could as the waves pushed them to shore along with the rest of the wreckage. So much debris had landed around them that it seemed like a ramshackle boardwalk of some kind they could have walked across.

༄

I surfaced riding huge waves and surrounded by debris, which fortunately gave me something to hang onto. Something hit me in the head when the wind threw it in my direction as the tornado disappeared over the steep bank to the east. I looked around and saw no one else—not one other person bobbing in the water. Panicked, I screamed, "God, save us!"

I looked toward the shoreline. *Where did that big pile of dirt come from?* I thought, before realizing it was the hillside. It was the complete absence of green that made it unrecognizable— almost every leaf and every pine needle had been stripped from the toppled trees. A few minutes before the entire hill had been green, covered in thick trees and lush undergrowth, with no bare ground showing anywhere. Now not a tree or cabin had been left standing onshore, and I didn't know where I was. I soon caught sight of Terry, Dale, and Shane several yards in front of me, and Priscilla in the water behind me. Immensely relieved, I realized I was not the only survivor!

When they reached shore, Terry and Dale carried Shane about 15 feet up the steep hill and laid him down. Dale's Boy Scout training kicked in. He ripped off his shirt, wrung it out, and used it as a compress for Shane's head.

"You'll be okay," they reassured Shane. Slivers, cuts, and bruises covered his arms.

This kid is going to die, Dale thought, *but we need to pretend that he's not.*

Dale tore off one pant leg to make a sling for Terry's hurting arm, which he thought was broken. Dale used the other pant leg to cover the cut over his own eye. Terry had lost his glasses. The teenagers looked at each other, covered in mud, bruises, and scrapes, and said, "What are we going to do?"

Dale had also believed they were the only survivors until he saw me and Priscilla being pushed to shore by the waves. Still in the water, I yelled to Terry and Dale, "I'm afraid Priscilla is going to have a miscarriage!"

"We're going to get help!" Terry called back. "We found Shane. He's up there." The two boys scrambled up the hillside to the gravel road. Fight or flight had settled in, and Terry suddenly had the urge to get out of there as quickly as possible.

They had a mind to find a car and drive to get help until they came across one of the Bethany station wagons with its windows blown out, wrapped in metal cables, and destroyed. There was no moving it, especially not with the trees littering the road. They continued toward the road on foot.

I pulled myself out of the water, walking across many feet of floating boards and cabin debris, and climbed the steep hill to where the boys had placed Shane. The six-year-old was unconscious by the time I got to him. His foot was bleeding so I took my cover-up belt off, wrapped it around his foot, and gently peeled Dale's shirt from his head to inspect his wound. What I saw scared me. His face was a mess, bruised and battered! The cut was so deep that I thought I could see the white of his skull. His eyes were blood red and the swelling of his face made him almost unrecognizable. I prayed for him, pleading with Jesus to save his life.

I proceeded back to the shoreline and helped Priscilla get out of the water a few minutes later. She stepped onto land, and she and I made our way over to Shane. A nail had scraped Priscilla in the shoulder. Her foot had also been cut, and she had many other minor abrasions; she looked pretty beat up.

Leaving Priscilla and Shane, I made it the rest of the way up the steep hill to the road. I was in a state of shock. A woman came walking down the road from the north and asked if I needed any help. The only thing that came to mind was that my swimsuit strap had broken, so she reached inside her dress and found a safety pin. We soon heard the buzz of chainsaws; people had already started clearing trees.

↜

Dick Dugan recounted the experience in his own words:

> "As I was pressed under the water by debris that final-ly began to lift, I struggled toward what I hoped would be the surface. With bursting lungs and a mind gripped with panic, I was certain I was going to die. Over and over the turbulent waters tumbled me until finally I just gave up and breathed in—and found air!

> Then—quicker than the storm had begun—it was gone. The swells on the lake lifted me as I gazed up at a beau-tiful clear blue sky. I was alive and I was exulting in the fact until, like a wave of nausea, exhaustion hit me. Des-perately I looked for something to support me, found a piece of lumber, and paddled feebly to shore.

> Priscilla was expecting our fourth child in just two months. Neither she nor any of the three children could

swim. I thought they all were gone. The wind had not blown us far, but the shoreline had changed radically— only a few twisted stumps stood where thick woods and cabins had been before. As I pulled myself up over fallen trees onto the shore, familiar faces began to appear."

Dick ran around the grounds looking for his five-year-old daughter, asking, "Has anybody seen Sharon? Has anybody seen Sharon?"

⌢

Returning from the hardware store in Emily, my dad Toby, brothers Lon and Jon, and cousin Sheila, looked over the lake to their west as they approached Outing. The pontoon boat that had been anchored 40 feet from shore when they first passed it was now onshore, like a huge hand had picked it up and transferred it to land. Once in town, they turned right at the intersection toward the cabins and noticed that the huge oak tree the post office had been nestled under now lay across its roof.

"Oh, no!" my dad exclaimed in disbelief.

They continued toward Sunset Hill Road, a gravel road east of town, until the number of downed trees prohibited them from driving any further. Before they could begin to get their bearings and figure out what on earth had happened, Terry and Dale appeared, crawling over fallen trees—Terry in swimming trunks, no shirt, blood on his chest. Dale, also shirtless, had a strip of cloth across his eye. "There's been a tornado! We have to get help!"

Quickly getting into the car, Dale exclaimed, "It's gone, everything is gone! It's been totally wiped out!"

"We don't know who's alive and who's dead," Terry added as they doubled back into town so my dad could make emergency

L to R: George Coughlin, Pat Coughlin, John Ramerth, Mike Ramerth

Above: Floyd and Thelma Simmons with daughter Jean in front of Lodge

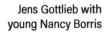

Jens Gottlieb with young Nancy Borris

Rae Knighton

George Zier

L to R: George and Betty Zier, Thelma and Floyd Simmons

Norma Borris and Nancy

George Zier and daughter Mary   Mary Zier with friend Roberta Munck

John and Norma Borris, Debbie and Nancy

Nancy Borris

Edith Dugan

Edith and Diane Dugan in a Bethany Cabin kitchen

Edith and Bernard Dugan in 1964

Diane Dugan and fiance Steve Dahlen in 1970

Terry

Diane

Terry Dugan and Sue Dugan, high school graduation, June 5, 1969

1969

Sue

Becky

Lon

Jon

Toby Dugan family,
June 5, 1969

Sue Dugan and Scott Moline, future husband

Ron

Don

Ken Dugan family,
August 1969

Ken Dugan with
Edith and Dorothy
Newton, Roosevelt
Lake 1967

Dick Dugan family 1967

Sharon

Priscilla

L to R: Sheila, Shane, Sharon

Shane and Sharon

Paul

Dan

Harold Brokke family 1967

Harold Carlson family at Darlene's wedding to David Anthony, June 1969

Dale

L to R: Harold and Evy Carlson,
Minnie and Rev. Arthur Olson

The New Village Singers:
Dan Brokke, Diane Dugan,
Dale Carlson, Terry Dugan

Tree cross, found near Long's cabin on Sunset Hill Road

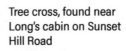

Harry and Olga Long, on his 75th birthday

Denise Gibis, Olga's granddaughter

Taylor family cabin, west shore of Roosevelt Lake

Tim Taylor (at left)

Jeanna, Dan and Pam Marko

L to R: Pam, Jeanna, Dan and Susan Marko

Sue, recovery diver Bill Matthies, Priscilla Dugan, diver Gary Fitch, July 2019

Survivors at the 2019 picnic—front row: Jeanna and Pam Marko, Cathy Brokke, Sheila (Dugan) Jensen, Priscilla Dugan, back row: Sue (Dugan) Moline, Lon Dugan, Diane (Dugan) Dahlen, Terry Dugan, Shane Dugan, Dan Brokke

calls. "We only saw Sue and Shane and Priscilla."

"Did you see my mom?" Jon said, terror written on his face. "Is my mom alive?"

"I don't remember seeing her," Terry replied.

"What about Becky?" Lon asked, "She can't swim!"

The older boys did not know.

They drove back to the little grocery and gas store in Outing. The owners let them use the store phone, and they began to make calls to the police, the ambulance, the fire department, and whoever else they could contact. Apparently, several other people had already made calls.

My dad left 12-year-old Lon at the store to direct emergency vehicles. Terry, Dale, Sheila, and Jon jumped back in the car and sped back to the lake.

"Stay in the car; it's dangerous," Toby told Sheila and Jon when they arrived. He made his way down the hill with Terry and Dale.

Lon patiently waited at the Outing store for two hours unnecessarily. All the emergency vehicles had driven to the resort on the other side of the lake without stopping at the store. Previous callers had given them the address of the Simmons Log Cabin Camp Resort, which was directly across the lake from the Bethany Cabins. No first responders came to our side of the lake.

⌐

By the time Dan managed to get Cathy and my sister, Becky, to the water's edge, Harold Brokke had been able to join in the rescue effort. Cathy's shorts had fallen off in the lake and she stood in her apron, clutching her cosmetics bag. My mom, Uncle Dick, and Aunt Barb began artificial respiration on Becky. Some rescue workers had arrived by boat and found Edith Dugan dead in the water.

Dan and Harold encountered a stranger, a young man neither of them knew, who helped bring a wounded Cathy up the steep bank to the road. When thinking about it over the years, Dan wondered if the stranger could have been an angel. It wasn't until I did the research for this book, almost fifty years after the event, that we discovered who this individual was. Twenty-one-year-old Tim Taylor was vacationing at his family's cabin about 200 yards north of the Simmons Log Cabin Camp Resort directly across the lake. His story is told in chapter eight.

ᑌᑎ

They found me walking aimlessly and encouraged me to get into the car that Cliff Barrager, the postmaster, had driven over to transport people to the hospital. Dan helped Cathy into the vehicle next to me.

"Don't worry, Mom, we'll find Paul," Dan reassured Cathy as he closed the back door.

He turned to me with terrible news. "Becky and your grandma, Edith, are dead. Paul and Sharon are still missing."

Cathy and I sat silently side-by-side in the back seat of the postmaster's car the entire twenty-five miles to the Crosby Hospital.

ᑌᑎ

Dan Brokke and Tim Taylor returned to the barren hillside, calling Paul's name. They had crossed the driveway and walked halfway down the hill toward where the rope swing had been when they stopped short. There, surrounded by fallen trees, were two female bodies.

Horrified, the young men looked at each other. The women had their arms wrapped around each other. Their bodies had been battered and mangled beyond recognition. It was something no one should ever have to see.

Dan didn't know what to do.

About an hour later, Harold and Darrell Carlson arrived, just returning from the shop where Arthur Olson's car had been dropped off for repairs. Darrell looked at Terry and his wounded brother Dale who were standing by, surveyed the wreckage, and cried out, "Where's my mom? Where's my mom?"

The young man broke down and wept.

Dan approached Harold Carlson. "There are two..." he tried to find the words to describe it, "...two...women down the hill." Suddenly it dawned on Dan that the dead women were probably Harold's wife, Evy, and her mom, Minnie Olson. "Don't go down there," Tim said to Darrell as he and Dan led Harold to where the bodies lay.

Minnie and Evy likely flew through the air clinging to each other and were mauled by the trees.

∽

After sitting in the car for a while, Jon decided to walk down to the lake, his nine-year-old mind concluding that this was an appropriate time to disobey his father and make sure his mom was alive. He carefully avoided stepping on live wires and other debris. He reached the shore and saw his dad, Toby, waist-deep in the water giving his sister, Becky, mouth-to-mouth resuscitation, surrounded by several other adults. Toby noticed him.

"Jon, get out of here!"

Jon scrambled back up the hill and sat down, distraught. Dan Brokke came over and put his arm around him.

"I—I think Becky might have gone to hell," Jon stammered.

"Why do you say that?"

"Because she was always disobeying Mom and Dad."

"Becky had a special problem and God knew about that," Dan said, "so don't worry."

Jon looked down at his hand. He still held the pixie sticks from his walk into town. Guilt washed over him and he tossed them aside—his way of telling the world that lives mattered more than candy.

"We laid her over the tree trunk and we breathed air into her mouth," my mom told a reporter.* My Uncle Dick was the last one to work on resuscitating Becky when my mom finally said, "Dick, she's gone."

⤺

By the evening of Wednesday, August 6, seven of the twenty-two people who went through the tornado at the Bethany property were either dead or missing. The two cabins at the bottom of the hill had been violently blown into the lake and the two cabins up on the road were also completely gone, blown into the woods across the road. Even Cabin 1 with its walkout basement had only nine cement blocks of its basement walls still standing. The destruction caused by the winds of the tornado in just over a minute was unbelievable.

The bodies of thirteen-year-old Paul Brokke and little five-year-old Sharon Dugan still had not been found. Rescue divers had been unsuccessful in their search to find them in the lake because of the dark, murky water. Rev. Arthur Olson was also still missing and presumed dead.

The steep driveway at the Bethany Cabins was impassable to emergency vehicles, as was much of Sunset Hill Road. Darrell Carlson's heavy Ford Galaxy 500 had blown down the driveway toward the lake, ending up on all-fours but with telephone wires wrapped around it. The car was now straddling the driveway two-thirds of the way down. Therefore, the bodies in the lake were transported by boats to a landing area near the bridge at the narrows.

*The Minneapolis Star, August 7, 1969

Edith's body was removed by boat first and Becky's body a little later; both had drowned.

CHAPTER SIX

Simmons Log Cabin Camp

Now I believe in Moses.
—Floyd Simmons

ronically, the only warning that [came to] many residents of the Outing area had originated in Backus [27 miles due West]. An unknown citizen reported a funnel sighting to Rollin Sycks, assistant Forester at Backus. Sycks radioed the information to State Forestry Headquarters at Park Rapids. Clint Converse, Forester at the Outing area, overheard the call on his radio, got the direction of the storm, and called Simmons Log Cabin at Outing."

"Mary Zier, daughter of camp owner George Zier, notified her father who in turn called Floyd Simmons, Outing Civil Defense Coordinator. Zier then got in his car and warned guests in the cabins at the resort to stay off the lake and be ready to take cover. Mr. Simmons had time to call eleven other Outing area residents before the approaching tornado forced him and Mrs. Simmons into the basement of their Roosevelt Lake home. It was destroyed."*

↩

Across the lake from the Bethany Cabins on the west shoreline of Roosevelt Lake sat Simmons Log Cabin Camp Resort, a family-owned resort of ten cabins and a lodge. George Zier had just bought the resort that spring from his uncle, Floyd Simmons, and moved his family up from Iowa to operate it. Floyd and his wife Thelma had moved into a house about a block south of the resort.

Saturdays were reserved for cleaning and preparing for the next group of guests, but the rest of the time George's 15-year-old daughter, Mary, swam and skied during the day and roasted marshmallows or played cards with the other young people in the evenings. The beginning of August was especially exciting because Roberta Munck, Mary's best friend from Iowa, came to stay with the Ziers for two weeks.

On August 6, Mary and Roberta returned to the resort around 4:00 p.m. after walking to Outing. The girls sat on the screened-in porch of the lodge visiting with Mary's mom, dad, and grandmother. Suddenly the phone rang. It was Floyd Simmons, who told George that he had just received a call from Clint Converse, the local forest ranger. A tornado was heading their direction from the west and it would be a good idea to warn the resort guests to stay off of the lake. George hopped in his truck and headed down the hill to notify the guests. Since northern Minnesota rarely saw tornadoes, Mary didn't think much of Floyd's warning.

George Zier arrived back at the lodge a few minutes later. The girls continued to visit on the porch as he stood by gazing west.

*Cass County Independent, August 14, 1969

Suddenly, he turned to his family.

"We're going to the basement!" Mary looked up to where her father had been staring. Black, swirling clouds filled the horizon. The Ziers quickly gathered their dog and the five of them headed down the stairs. It wasn't long until they heard a train-like roar thundering over their heads.

"We're going into the fruit cellar!" George yelled over the sound.

He hurried them into the tiny room off of the basement. George gripped the cellar door handle as the wind tried to wrench it out of his hands.

Silence returned in a matter of minutes. The door was still.

George opened the fruit cellar door and proceeded to the bottom of the basement steps, the women and girls following close behind. They saw blue sky at the top of the stairway. George led the way up.

Mary burst into tears as she took in the devastation. The entire roof of the lodge had been swept away. The tall, beautiful pines that surrounded it had disappeared, leaving the ground completely barren. Without the trees, the family could see all the way to where Floyd and Thelma's house no longer stood, about a block south of the resort. George immediately took off running down the dirt road to find them.

He could see straight down into his aunt and uncle's basement, and there was the couple, unharmed and huddled in a corner. They had watched in amazement through a basement window as the wind roared and witnessed what looked like two tornadoes slam into each other in the middle of the lake. The tornado scooped up so much water that Floyd saw the lake bottom!

"Now I believe in Moses," Floyd later told his children.

George helped Floyd and Thelma climb out of the remains of their basement and returned to the resort. He went from cabin to cabin and discovered that four of the ten cabins were completely destroyed and all of them sustained some damage. Several guests had been injured and tragically, two guests in Cabin 8 had been killed.

Mary and Roberta stood still amidst the chaos, shock gluing their feet to the dirt. A few odd things still remained: the cake pan from the cake Mary's mother had just baked sat on the kitchen counter, but the cake had been sucked out of the pan. The three-paned glass door out to the porch, which the Ziers used to check in new guests, still had the middle pane intact. Fortunately, the church down the road had not been touched.

Cabin 1 guest, Mack Hunt, soon ran around the resort yelling "Don't smoke! Don't smoke!" He worked for the gas company and was worried about LP gas explosions. His family of seven had huddled under the big oak table in Cabin 1 as the tornado passed over. The south wall and part of the roof were torn away, but the family survived unharmed. Youngest son Jim, age 7, remembers someone opening a kitchen cupboard and the wall behind it was missing, but the dishes still sat on the cupboard shelves. Soon doors were being removed from the rubble to use as stretchers.

Several guests were transported to the Crosby Hospital by residents of the surrounding towns that had stopped along the highway and offered to help.

Special satellite phones allowed the Ziers to get in touch with other family and friends. Mary's brother, stationed at the U. S. Air Force base in Okinawa, Japan, saw the tornado on the news before the Ziers could reach him and got an emergency leave to help with the aftermath. The day he got to the property, the National Guard wouldn't let him in. He waited there in his Air Force uniform until George arrived and told the guard he was family.

Later, the couple staying in Cabin 4 with their parents and other family members told of the young dad and baby being picked up and thrown out of the cabin, yet remained unharmed. The dad had found the baby lying on top of a mattress close by and amazingly, completely fine.

Pontoons had been ripped in two and canoes had been torn to pieces. The Ziers could see straight across the lake to where the Bethany Cabins had been—the cabins had disappeared.

CHAPTER SEVEN

Resort Guests

*With a jerk the cabin started to move, the walls
collapsing as it turned on its side.*

It was the third or fourth year that young Nancy Borris's family
had spent their summer vacation at Simmons Log Cabin Camp
Resort—always requesting the same two cabins—7 and 8. They
loved the resort and the little lakeside cabins. They looked forward
to a week with grandparents, Jens and Julie Gottlieb, and Aunt Rae
Knighton, her mother's favorite sister. They were a very close family.

Nancy was nine in the summer of 1969, going into third
grade. Her family, John and Norma Borris and her older sister,
Debbie, age 11, rented Cabin 7, while her grandparents and aunt
rented Cabin 8. The 600-square foot cabins were identical, each

with two bedrooms, a bathroom, an open kitchen, a living room area, and a screened-in porch. They sat side-by-side at the bottom of the hill 50 or 60 feet from the west shoreline of Roosevelt Lake, directly across the bay from the Bethany Cabins.

On the evening of Wednesday, August 6, they were having guests for dinner and the women were busy cooking in Cabin 8, where they all gathered. Milo Mielke and his wife had arrived from across the lake to enjoy the evening with the entire family.

Just before suppertime, a few minutes just shy of 5:00 p.m., there was an urgent knock on the cabin door, which Nancy answered. There stood a man who looked like a state trooper, coming to warn them that a bad storm was coming. She closed the door and almost immediately the wind picked up and heavy rain began. Aunt Rae ran into the bedrooms to close the windows and Nancy followed her. A white mass was blowing by outside the windows— almost like snow. This, she realized, was the approaching storm. Nancy's mom yelled to her girls to get behind the kitchen counter. It would have made no difference.

With a jerk the cabin started to move, the walls collapsing as it turned on its side. The roof flew off as the storm blew the little cabin off its foundation. Nancy saw her aunt's head strike the walls three quick times as the cabin blew apart. The vacationers were blown to the north as the cabin was completely destroyed. Nancy landed on her aunt's body, which was face down. Aunt Rae had not survived the repeated blows to her head and Nancy did not turn her over.

Horrified, she saw her Grandpa Jens lying on the ground with his eyes open and knew he was gone too, also killed by head trauma. Nancy ran down to the lake and, at first, saw nothing and no one. Then other family members who had survived began moving around. Mrs. Mielke was found trapped under a wall, injured but blessedly alive. Grandma Julie suffered only a goose egg on her head but was wrapped in power lines around her waist. She remembered seeing the water suctioned out of the lake and boats flying by above the water.

Nancy, wearing cut-offs and a Minnesota Twins t-shirt that day, had been sandblasted by the storm. She was covered with sand—it was even imbedded in her skin for weeks afterward. The large gash in her right thigh would need stitches.

In a state of shock, she meandered around the property, helping other resort guests as much as a nine-year-old could. She assisted a very pregnant woman to lie down on the ground and put a wet washcloth on her head.

Nancy's dad, John, had been hanging onto the screen door as the cabin disintegrated. He was treated in the Crosby Hospital and released, but somehow the medical staff missed the many broken ribs in his chest, allowing him to drive his family home the following day. When the doctors wanted to suture the deep cut on Nancy's thigh, she was frightened and refused the treatment. Her mother, Norma, in a state of shock by the sudden death of her father and her sister (her best friend) responded, "Whatever she says." No sutures were done.

Rae Knighton, age 55, and her father Jens Gottlieb, age 87, were the first two casualties of this monster storm as it blew from west to east across Roosevelt Lake.

Cabin 7, the Borris family's cabin just a few feet away from Cabin 8, was damaged but not demolished.

Grandma Julie had taken off her wedding ring while doing the dishes in the kitchen and set it up on the windowsill. A week later, she sent one of her sons and two grandsons back to the resort to look for it. They decided to humor her, quite sure they would never find it. Arriving at the demolished resort near where the cabin had been, they stopped their car and opened the door. There, sparkling on the ground right next to the car, was her ring. A message from Grandpa Jens to his wife? The family liked to think so.

CHAPTER EIGHT

"Angel" in Disguise

The one amazing sight I most vividly recall is watching all the trees just fold down in unison. Literally, hundreds of trees just bent down to the ground, not breaking, but lying down with their tree roots, with all the soil, just lifting up from underneath the ground.

—TIM TAYLOR

Tim Taylor was relaxing alone at his family's rustic cabin overlooking Roosevelt Lake's west shoreline—his parents, aunt, and uncle had left the cabin a few days earlier. Tim was 21 and about to start his senior year of college. He really enjoyed the cool fresh water of Roosevelt Lake, swimming across it a couple of times a day.

On August 6, he was swimming about 100 yards offshore when the sky turned an ominous shade of yellow from the approaching storm. He quickly swam to shore, sprinted up the concrete steps to the cabin on the hill, and dove under the bed in the living room. But he couldn't resist sticking his head out to peer through the windows.

Suddenly, he saw hundreds of trees tipped down in unison, bending to the ground as if a giant hand had leveled them. Even the three huge white pines that had survived a forest fire years earlier lay flat against the dirt.

The old cabin creaked from the extreme pressure but did not explode. The garage and boathouse also held fast, although their aluminum boat eventually came to rest up in a tree.

After the wind subsided, Tim emerged from under the bed and stepped onto the porch, amazed to see how close Simmons Resort really was to his cabin. His family had never been able to see the resort before because of all the trees. Now that they were flattened, he had clear visibility.

Tim climbed over logs and debris toward the resort. Guests walked around with dazed expressions, incredulous that they were alive. He looked east across the lake to where the Bethany Cabins had been. Only the concrete foundations remained.

Then Tim remembered seeing three teenagers from the Bethany Cabins in a canoe a few times while he swam. Two had been paddling at each end while a girl, who appeared mentally disabled, sat in the middle.

They had waved and said, "Hello," and he felt like he knew them in a way. That minor connection with the girls prompted Tim to check for survivors on the other side of the lake.

He found a man who had a car and they drove south on Highway 6, across the bridge at the narrows and as far as they could through Outing. When they reached the east side of Roosevelt

Lake, downed trees obstructed the road making it impossible to go any further. Tim ran the rest of the way to the Bethany property clear to the bottom of the steep driveway.

A partially-submerged tree trunk floated in the water and on it a girl lay; someone was giving her mouth-to-mouth resuscitation, her face purple. Tim recognized my sister Becky as the one who sat in the middle of the canoe. Tim was experienced in mouth-to-mouth and tried resuscitating her, as did several others, but it was too late. He saw a petite older woman—Edith Dugan—floating face down in the water and helped hoist her body into a small boat.

That was when Tim encountered Dan Brokke and they discovered the bodies of the other two women. It was gut-wrenching to watch Harold Carlson identify his wife and mother-in-law. His teenage son Darrell stood up on the road with tears in his eyes.

Tim overheard that five-year-old Sharon Dugan was still un-accounted for. A strong swimmer and college lifeguard, Tim spent at least an hour diving underwater to look for her, feeling under fallen debris in case she had been trapped. Every time he felt some-thing soft, he desperately hoped it wasn't her. No one found Sharon on Wednesday.

Later that evening, Tim hitchhiked a ride to Emily, the next town south, and found a payphone to call his parents. They had heard about the storm and were worried sick about him. His uncle drove up to the cabin the next day and together they began the massive task of clearing downed trees.

CHAPTER NINE

The Lake Turned Upside Down

The wind had scooped up the entire lake and dropped it down again.

—Patrick Baier

Four lots south of the Bethany Cabins on Sunset Hill Road, eleven-year-old Bobby Kleinschmidt and his family hid in their basement as the tornado hit their property. Like Bethany Cabins 1 and 2, their cabin was also located high above the lake on top of the bluff, 40 feet or so above lake level. The entire cabin was picked up and thrown across the road. Eight people were staying in the cabin at the time—the Kleinschmidts and their guests, the Ivers. Running into the basement saved the lives of these two mothers and six kids, but the tornado sucked the wood stairway out of the basement, forcing the group to climb out on all fours.

Bobby looked toward the lake and saw huge waves leaping up

and down in no particular direction. No one in their group had sustained any injuries worse than minor cuts and scratches.

Since the hordes of fallen trees made it impossible to go any-where, the families had no idea, until the next day, that so many people had been hurt and killed just a few lots north of them.

↜

Sixteen-year-old Lynn Rogers, born and raised in Outing, was working at the Lakeview Store that afternoon. The store faced Roo-sevelt Lake just south of the Highway 6 bridge. Her boss had just received a call from someone in Pine River and told her to get in the storage basement and stay there—a tornado was coming! She did that for about ten seconds then, being sixteen and invincible, went back upstairs to the front windows that faced Roosevelt Lake. She saw a lady in her car at the gas pumps, clutching her steering wheel with a terrified look on her face. Her boss was trying to get to the lady, but the pressure from the tornado would not allow him to open the door.

As Lynn watched through the front window, a wall of dark clouds came down the lake and the water in the lake lifted up, to-tally exposing the sandy bottom. Debris was flying everywhere! Then, just as quickly as it had started, it stopped.

↜

The Baier family cabin sat on the northeast side of Roosevelt Lake at the very tip of the lake, about 2½ miles north of the Bethany Cabins. From their cabin, they had a clear view down the long narrow north end of the lake. In the first week of August, they had many extended family members staying with them.

Late afternoon on August 6, they saw bad weather moving in their direction and watched with great interest. Fourteen-year-old Pat Baier had to use the bathroom and missed seeing the tornado, but when he came into the living room, his mom told him that the wind had *scooped up the entire lake* and dropped it down again. The sight so shocked her she claimed she wet her pants.

Fortunately, their cabin had not sustained any damage. After the family decided it was safe and with his dad's permission, Pat, his brother-in-law, and a neighbor took their boat out on the lake to see if they could help anyone. They encountered lots of debris; cabin roofs floated past their boat as they sped along. When they came by Johnson Point, the site of the Bethany Cabins was vacant—like the lakeside cabins had never existed.

They continued south on the lake and as they approached the bridge they saw a sheriff's boat towing the body of a girl—with a rope around her neck. The sheriff told the group it was an eighteen-year-old girl who had drowned. It was my sister Becky. The sheriff was alone in a 14-foot fishing boat and he had been unable to get Becky's body into the boat by himself.

It was an unpleasant experience for Pat who had never seen a dead body before. He could tell that the Sheriff felt terrible about transporting Becky's body the way he did, but he was alone in his boat and had no other choice.

Pat's brother-in-law helped the sheriff carry Becky's body up onto the shore. Pat saw my mom, Vonnie, talking to the sheriff and confirming the identity of her daughter. My brother Jon arrived and took in the scene. Jon approached our mom and tapped her arm. Becky's body was lying under a tree, covered by a blanket.

"Mom, this is exactly what I saw in my dream," Jon said.

CHAPTER 10

Neighbors on the Bluff

The Longs' white, newly renovated cabin had been demolished—even the cement block walkout basement was destroyed.

A cabin sat next to Edith Dugan's at the top of the hill, one lot to the north, belonging to Harry and Olga Long, an elderly couple and longtime Outing summer vacationers. On August 6, Olga, an excellent cook and baker, stood in her kitchen preparing food for a dinner party with friends that evening, Mr. and Mrs. George Ginn, and perhaps one other couple. Another friend, Katherine Rotar, was going to stop by later for dessert. The Ginns and Rotars were neighbors on the lake about a quarter of a mile south of the Longs' cabin.

Olga Long's granddaughter, seventeen-year-old Denise Gibis,

was vacationing up north that week with her friend Suzie. The two girls stopped by the Longs' cabin earlier in the day on Wednesday and promised to come back later to swim. Denise had not seen her grandmother since her high school graduation that summer and was excited to spend some time with her.

Later that afternoon, the girls borrowed Suzie's brother's car to drive back to the Longs' cabin. As they crossed the bridge in the town of Crosslake, Suzie accidentally down-shifted the manual vehicle into reverse and wrecked the transmission. They pushed the car to a gas station on the other side of the bridge to get it repaired. As they waited, ambulances from Brainerd sped through the town on their way to Outing. The girls had no idea why.

Fortunately, Denise and Suzie never made it back to Outing—without the car trouble, they would have arrived at the Longs' cabin just about the time the tornado hit.

↬

The wind picked up right before the Ginns planned to leave their cabin for dinner with the Longs. Because of the threatening weather, the couple opted to climb into their storm shelter below the kitchen and wait it out before going to the Longs' cabin on the high bluff above the lake. Other than one or two trees, the storm left the Ginn's property virtually untouched.

↬

Katherine Rotar had decided to eat an early dinner with her two daughters and three grandchildren and then go to the Longs' cabin a little later for dessert. The tornado hit as the Rotars sat at the dinner table. Katherine's eight-year-old granddaughter Patricia looked across Roosevelt Lake and watched clouds rolling in across a blue sky. When the white birch trees in front of the cabin split in two, she saw the tornado approaching their cabin.

Katherine pushed a rollaway against the window, desperately trying to keep the rain from entering through the porch windows. The Rotars dashed down into the cellar through the trap door in the floor—they never would have made it down in time if they'd used the outside cellar door. Patricia's dog hid under a chair and refused to come down into the cellar, so Patricia ran away from her mother to grab the dog.

"Get back down!" Katherine yelled as Patricia was transfixed by the sight out the window. The tornado pounded straight through the lake, cutting the water down the middle like the parting of the Red Sea. Debris spun around the dry bottom of the lake as the tornado headed directly toward the Rotars's cabin. Patricia stood frozen in place until her grandmother pulled her back into the cellar.

Their cabin was well-built out of concrete blocks, yet the tornado lifted the entire thing up four inches and dropped it back down. The Rotars watched the bottom of the funnel pass over the cellar's north air vent, the wind screeching horrifically. The family said the Hail Mary and the Lord's Prayer over and over, certain they were about to die.

Just as quickly as it came, the storm disappeared and the cellar got eerily quiet. Katherine and her family pushed aside the chairs the wind had blown over the cellar trap door and climbed up into the kitchen. It was a mess. All the porch windows were blown out and broken glass covered the floor. Patricia looked at the dinner table. Strangely, the napkins in the napkin holder were still in place. Both the east and west walls had cracked from floor to ceiling, leaving a quarter-inch gap in between.

The family walked outside and was amazed to see the cabin had shifted two inches off its foundation. Even the concrete slab outside the cabin doorway was displaced. The metal lawn chairs had been tossed into the woods, but the webbed lawn chairs remained in their usual places around the fire pit. Huge century-old trees had been snapped in half.

The lake weeds were shoved about four feet up the shoreline, and the children ran around throwing fish back into the lake, many of them huge!

All of the Rotars' neighbors sustained damage. In spite of the trees and debris blocking the roadways, the sheriff was able to make his way down to their area on foot to see if anyone needed emergency medical attention. Fortunately, a retired medical doctor that lived at the end of the road had already treated the minor cuts and scrapes.

With nothing to do and no way to contact anyone, Katherine and her family nailed sheets and blankets over the open windows and tried to rest that night. Patricia's uncle drove to Outing as soon as he heard about the tornado, banging on the cabin door when he arrived in the middle of the night. He had heard about fatalities and didn't know what to expect as he hurried from the highway to the cabin.

↬

Bud Roach was a St. Paul firefighter with a family cabin just a few lots south of the Ginn and Rotar cabins, on O'Brien Road. On August 6, he rushed home from town when the weather started to get bad, only to find that his wife and children were already in the cabin with the door jammed shut from the changing pressure, as if locked. With no other option, he decided to take refuge under his car and was facing the lake as the tornado blew over.

He heard a sound and watched the neighbor's boathouse lift up and head toward his car, but it ended up wrapped around a tree.

Then he saw a boat go sailing by about ten feet above the water. As he looked across the lake to a huge stand of pine trees, he saw the top one-third of the trees all snap off at once and shoot away like they had been shot out of a gun.

Bud was one of the first responders to reach the site of the devastation just a block or two north of his cabin. Later that evening, he also accompanied his neighbor George Ginn up the steep hill to check on Harry and Olga Long. When George became exhausted from the climb and could not walk any further, Bud continued on about twenty more feet and found the body of Harry Long.

⌒

The Longs' white, newly renovated cabin had been demolished—even the cement block walkout basement was destroyed. Stan Johnson, the owner of the Outing lumberyard and hardware store, went searching for his friends, the Longs, after the storm blew through. They had visited his hardware store just that afternoon, perhaps preparing for their dinner party with friends that evening.

Stan found Olga about a city block back in the woods, across the road from where their cabin had stood. She was alive but pinned underneath a tree, and according to a local story, still clinging to her cooking utensils. The tornado had hit their cabin so suddenly they did not even have time to head to their walkout basement.

Olga was taken to Crosby Hospital after someone cut the tree away, where she later passed away. Harry was found lying along Sunset Hill Road. His death had been immediate, caused by shock from multiple fractures, according to his death certificate. Stan and others covered his head.

Anatomy of a Tornado

Along the road were trees that had been twisted halfway up their trunks. Not just blown down, but twisted like a piece of wool yarn.
—Barb Grove, *Cuyuna Country—A People's History*

Understanding the anatomy of this tornado helps to explain why our cabin blew into the lake instead of being smashed into pieces on the hillside.

I mentioned earlier that the three newer Bethany Cabins were built up on cement block footings rather than on cement slabs. There was at least a foot, probably more, of open space between the floor of the cabin and the ground. Cabins 3 and 4 at the bottom of the hill, on the peninsula, were facing roughly north and the F4 tornado was blowing from west to east.

Tornadoes spin in a counter-clockwise direction and this was a very large wedge tornado, a mile to a mile and a half wide. It hit us very near the core or the center of the tornado, with wind speeds up to 260 mph. Those high rotating winds blew under our cabin from behind, lifted it up off the footings, and blew us north–northwest into the lake. The well-built cabin hung together in one piece until it hit the wall of water in the lake. Although four people in our cabin drowned, thirteen of us were saved by the water. The wind speed and direction had to be perfect for us to hit the water and not the steep hill and trees.

There is a possibility that Cabin 4, which was unoccupied at that time, might not have broken into pieces when it entered the lake. There are stories about a complete cabin sitting on the bottom of the lake. One of them came from George Carleton, a 26-year-old who lived on a farm in Emily. George was one of the first responders to the disaster area, armed with an axe, a chain saw, and a gallon of gas, working for days on both sides of the lake in search and rescue.

Three to four years after the tornado, he was on Roosevelt Lake in his boat (a hydroplane) when he saw a dive flag. A diver surfaced and wanted to show him something, so George put on some gear, dove down, and saw a complete cabin sitting on the bottom. He thinks the roof was still on, but he's not sure—but he remembers a toilet seat hanging on the front of the cabin, like a decorative wreath. That is what stuck in his memory. He guessed the cabin was about 20 feet x 24 feet.

⌒

This tornado picked up a huge amount of water and then dropped it down again. I heard from at least four eyewitnesses that they saw the lake bottom during the storm. I recently heard a story that a stream that runs into the north end of the lake became a waterfall for a short time and loggers even found dead fish in the woods *five miles away* from the nearest lake.

Leavitt Lake

Just about the time the last piece of debris was hitting me in the head as the tornado disappeared over the hill to the east, time was running out for Leavitt Lake. Leavitt is about one mile east of Roosevelt Lake and was a well-populated lake with many summer cabins. The lake is roughly two miles long and lies in a southwest-to-northeast direction, exactly the path of the tornado.

On Leavitt Lake, the trees told the story. The tornado roared right down the middle of the lake and across both shorelines, leaving the trees lying down in one direction on the south side and the opposite direction on the north side.

⌒

The four Zagar sisters were home alone at their cabin on Leavitt Lake while their mom, Betty Zagar, was doing the wash in Emily. The girls, Katy, Carol, Mary, and Marge ranged in age from nine to fifteen, and were watching the *I Love Lucy Show* when the TV suddenly turned to black and white lines.

Katy, the oldest, told the girls to get to the corner of the living room, along with their dog Penny. She had read a *TV Guide* article just the week before on how to take shelter in the event you are in a home without a basement when a tornado strikes.

According to Marge, the youngest, the sound of the tornado has never left her memory. "It sounded like a freight train. Everything was pulled from under us and then thrown upon us. We all survived, including Penny. When we woke up power lines were everywhere. Our biggest fear was that the lines would kill us.

Miracles happened that day for my family."

Carol remembers that they "were dropped in what was left of the footings of the newly added addition. My sister Mary was picked up and dropped in the kitchen sink on the few remaining cupboards because she broke away from our huddle in the corner of the addition to run and save our dog Penny!"

They escaped with cuts and bruises, but they lost almost everything. Their pontoon boat flew from land into the lake upside down, and their mom's hairpiece was in a tree. Emergency responders helped them find their parents.

A picture of the Zagar's cabin wall with the clock stopped at the time the tornado struck, just before 5:00 p.m., was on the front page of the *Minneapolis Star* on August 8, 1969, the headline reading "Then time ran out..."

There were many injuries and tremendous damage at Leavitt Lake, but fortunately no deaths.

Lawrence Lake

It was also laundry day at the Ashcraft cabin on Lawrence Lake— just south of Leavitt Lake and east of Outing. Thirteen-year-old Carol was in charge of her younger sisters while her parents and older sister were in town at the Laundromat. It was a very strange weather day—sunny and hot, but with big white clouds rolling across the sky and lots of thunder—causing her some concern about the weather.

When her parents and sister returned, Carol's dad immediately walked down the hill to the lakeshore instead of coming into the cabin. Then he rushed through the door and shouted "Come on, we've got to get out of here!" They all ran to a ditch near their driveway and stacked on top of each other in the low-lying area, little ones on the bottom and her parents on top. Her dad told them a huge tornado was heading across the lake right toward them.

Carol remembers, "It turned as dark as the darkest night and we could hear the tornado, like a train, going by. We were all praying together and at one point I heard my dad say to my mom, 'Mom, how are we going to save these kids?'" At that moment she knew their lives were in real danger and she also understood the depth of her dad's love for his family.

When the tornado passed, their cabin was still standing, but trees were down all over. Her dad cut a path to the highway with his chain saw and they were stunned at what they saw. "We knew Leavitt Lake was on the other side of the road, but that day we could see all of Leavitt Lake and for miles beyond. The entire face of the land was changed in those several minutes."

CHAPTER 12

Search and Rescue

*That night I rode for a time with a man who had a
vehicle from the funeral home. I was an R. N. and we
went about back roads. That night was terrifying.
There were no injuries found but what I remember in
that car ride through long dark roads was the
sound of chain saws. I was afraid to sleep that night.
I believed the peace of the lake was gone forever.*
—ELLEN LEGER, WASHBURN LAKE

According to Jim Dowson, a twenty-nine-year-old Cass County Chief Deputy Sheriff at that time, the sheriff's department and emergency responders arrived at the devastating scene near Outing within 15 or 20 minutes after the storm blew through. They were aware of storm warnings and already knew a tornado had hit Backus, but unfortunately, there were no warning sirens in the Outing area to announce the direction it was headed. More dangerously, the storm was moving very fast—55-60 miles an hour.

The town of Outing had no fire department, so rescuers came to help out from Remer, Emily, Crosslake, and Brainerd. Most fire trucks were equipped with only one chain saw per vehicle, but were joined by hundreds of residents who had chain saws, and several hardware stores started giving chain saws away.

The first responders arrived on the west side of Roosevelt Lake first and from there saw the complete devastation on the east shore where the Bethany Cabins had stood. The problem was getting in there with the roads blocked by downed trees, but it was imperative that they get a dive team started right away. They called on some local divers from the Walker area and then contacted the Minnesota Para Rescue team from Minneapolis to come that night.

The tornado had stayed on the ground for 38 miles destroying thousands of acres of forest, and they were certain that many injured or trapped cabin owners were in those woods. They also knew of the missing persons from the Bethany property on the east side of Roosevelt Lake.

The Minnesota governor, Harold Levander, quickly declared the situation a disaster area and called in the National Guard. Outing's Town Hall transformed into a command center and security checkpoint and everyone in and out of the area had to have a badge stating who they were and why they were there. Looters arrived on the scene almost immediately, as did news stations with cameras, and worried family members wondering if their loved ones were safe. All electricity and phone services were out for miles around.

Highway 6 going north out of Outing became a temporary landing strip for airplanes. The Civil Air Patrol was activated with their Duck boat (amphibious truck) and airplanes, looking for survivors. Residents on the lake also searched, looking under floating cabin debris.

Eventually, the Cass County Sheriff's Department requested the DNR to fly over the area to give the ground people a description of what was happening and to follow the path of the tornado. Several planes were dispatched to make sure all the injured people in the woods and cabins were rescued.

As it grew dark that evening, the Civil Air Patrol was still flying and searching. Over one area of destroyed woods, the pilots saw a flashing light down below and called in a search and rescue team. The rescuers worked their way toward the flashing light, hoping to help the stranded people. When they arrived, they found only the open trunk of a car flapping in the wind, exposing the trunk light off and on.

The local ladies set up a food station at the Town Hall and began making sandwiches for the rescuers. The Red Cross and the Salvation Army were also there helping out with food. Shirley Johnson, owner of the Outing hardware store with her husband Stan, remembers going into the grocery store and grabbing off the shelves everything they could possibly use for sandwiches and meals. Shirley had received the 11th phone call from Floyd Simmons, who yelled "a tornado's coming!" before slamming down his phone and heading to his basement.

The ladies worked tirelessly around the clock for many days. According to Deputy Sheriff Dowson, "The rescuers got treated royally with all the ladies in town cooking and baking!"

Minnesota Para Rescue Team

The Minnesota Para Rescue team, a volunteer group of highly-trained rescue specialists, was called to Outing on Wednesday evening by the Cass County Sheriff's Department and transported by state rescue vehicles. Phil Halper was the captain of the all-volunteer team.

All members of the team were ex-Army Airborne paratroopers. All were certified EMT instructors, American Red Cross instructors, certified SCUBA divers, high-level rescue instructors, winter survival instructors, extrication instructors, and state PRIM (Professional Rescue Instructors of Minnesota). They were all active skydivers at the time as well and were on call 24/7.

They arrived in Outing about 11:00 p.m. on August 6. Soon after the team's arrival, an elderly lady named Isabelle Busby entered the command center covered in scratches. She had somehow cut her way out of the woods with an axe and a buck saw. She said the tornado had destroyed her cabin and one of her grandchildren was missing out at Reservoir Lake, eight miles northeast of town.

Two Para Rescue team members immediately made their way back to Reservoir Lake to rescue her family and search for her missing granddaughter. The rest of the team went to Roosevelt Lake where volunteers had cut a path through the debris down to the shoreline. The team started to dive early the morning of Thursday, August 7 and dove most of the day. They found the lake bottom cluttered with cabins, cars, and everything else that had been on the lakeshore.

At about 8:00 a.m. Thursday morning, the Para Rescue team divers found the body of Rev. Arthur Olson in ten feet of water. He had lost his pants, and the team performed the complicated task of placing his body in a recovery bag while underwater to keep it out of sight from the news cameras onshore. Although he was found in the lake, his cause of death was a broken neck and a crushed chest. He had probably been flung 75-plus feet from their cabin on the hill into the lake.

Reservoir Lake

Eleanor Marko and her four children, Dan, Pamela, Jeanna, and Susan, had been vacationing with her mother, Isabelle Busby, at her remote Reservoir Lake cabin, the only cabin on that lake. Eleanor, recently divorced, was adjusting to being a single mom to four little children, ages two to nine. They had spent several weekends at the lake that summer, and now the first week of August were staying the entire week.

After picking raspberries Wednesday afternoon, August 6, Isabelle brought the family back to the cabin for supper. She then returned by car to picking berries by herself, and fortunately missed the storm. As the tornado was approaching the cabin, the kids hid under the bunk beds, but the roof blew off, the walls came down, and the entire family was blown out of the cabin.

The smallest children were blown the farthest. Pam (5) and Jeanna (3) "came to" with their feet in the lake. Nine-year-old Dan landed about halfway between the girls and their mother, Eleanor, who had been blown halfway to the lake and was unable to move because of her injuries. Two-year-old Susan was missing.

When Isabelle attempted to return to her cabin, she found that the storm had left the road and long driveway impassable. She left her car on the highway with a note on the windshield and cut her way back to the cabin with an axe and a buck saw, where she found her daughter and grandkids, but was unable to find the youngest, Susan. Somehow Isabelle managed to get them all into the cab of a pickup truck to prevent shock from setting in, and then went for help, arriving at the Outing command center shortly after 11:00 p.m. By this time, almost six hours had passed since the tornado had devastated her property.

Two members of the Para Rescue team returned to the site at

Reservoir Lake with Isabelle. They too could not find Susan that evening. Of the other three grandchildren, nine-year-old Dan Marko was injured the most severely, needing 115 stitches in his head. Dan and five-year-old Pam were carried out on the backs of rescue workers around midnight. About 1:00 a.m., an ambulance was finally able to reach the site and rescue Eleanor and three-year-old Jeanna. Eleanor was very seriously injured, with a compound fracture of her leg, broken ribs, dislocated arms and internal injuries. She subsequently spent weeks in the hospital in traction.

Susan Marko had been swept into the lake, but her death had been immediate from a broken neck. Her little body was found in shallow water on Thursday by a member of the Minnesota Para Rescue team.

Two-year-old Susan Marko became the twelfth victim of the Outing tornado.

↩

The State Patrol ran steady trips to Brainerd to keep the team in air tanks. They were relieved by local divers in the late afternoon on August 7. The Minnesota Para Rescue team left on Thursday to return to the Twin Cities, having found the bodies of Susan Marko and Arthur Olson.

↩

Students from the University of Minnesota came up to help with the cleanup, as well as a group of Mennonite men from northwest Minnesota, equipped with hand tools. The Mennonites worked like machines, clearing trees twice as fast as their supervisor's bulldozer.

A volunteer group of hippies from the Twin Cities caused a stir when they were discovered skinny-dipping in Washburn Lake after a hard day of work.

Bethany cabins #3 and #4 before the tornado

Bethany property after the storm, looking from cabin #4 location toward the east shoreline

Bethany cabin #2 at the top of the hill

Bethany driveway, all cabins gone above and below

Simmons cabins #7 and #8 before the tornado

A damaged Simmons cabin

Looking toward the destroyed
Bethany property from
Simmons'

Simmons resort shoreline

Simmons resort destruction

The Long cabin demolished—local girl Margaret Olds sitting on the rubble

Harry and Olga Long's cabin before

Simmons cabin # 8 before, and after
(at right)

Simmons resort in foreground, Bethany cabins across the lake

Sunset Hill Road just south
of Bethany cabins

Aerial photo of the tornado's path

Aerial photos courtesy of the
Minnesota DNR

The Minneapolis STAR

Thursday, Aug. 7, 1969   Four Sections   10c

12 known dead in tornadoes

Camps near Outing hit worst by storms

Tornado Victims Listed

Here is a list of the known dead in the tornadoes which hit northern Minnesota Wednesday:

Killed at Bethany Fellowship Camp, Roosevelt Lake, near Outing:

1. The Rev. Arthur S. Olson, in 70's, 7021 Augsburg Ave., Richfield.
2. Mrs. Arthur S. Olson, in 70's, same address.
3. Mrs. Harold Carlson, in 50s, daughter of Olsons, 6820 Auto Club Rd., Bloomington.
4. Mrs. Edith Dugan, 62, 6820 Auto Club Rd., Bloomington.
5. Rebecca Ann Dugan, 6820 Auto Club Rd., Bloomington.

Killed at Simmons Log

Cabin Camp, Roosevelt Lake:

6. Mrs. Rae J. Knighton, 53, 5800 Meadow Lake Rd. W., New Hope.
7. Jens Gottleib, about 80, 2727 Lincoln St. N.E., Minneapolis.

Killed at nearby cottage, Roosevelt Lake.

8. Harry Long, about 65, 1029 Stryker Ave., West St. Paul
9. Mrs. Harry Long, same address.

Killed at Reservoir Lake, Outing:

10. Susan Marks, 2, 3035 Virginia Ave., St. Louis Park.

Killed at Boulder Lake, north of Duluth:

11. Mrs. Dennis Hietala, 32, Duluth.

Killed in Aitkin County:

12. Mrs. Arthur Hietala, 56, rural Aurora, Minn.

Killed at Atkin County:

13. John Dahl, 75, Ball Bluff.

42 Hospitalized After Tornadoes

Forty-two tornado victims were hospitalized Thursday at Itasca Hospital in Grand Rapids, St. Luke's in Duluth, Chisholm Memorial, Cuyuna Range District Hospital at Crosby, St. Joseph's in Brainerd and University of Minnesota Hospitals in Minneapolis.

Those from the Twin Cities

Mrs. Carol Batey, 34, Charlton, Iowa, fair
Kathy Chalich, 17, Backus, back injuries.
Barbara Chalich, 10, Backus, good.
Mark Holden, 18, Backus, good.

The dead:

At Simmons Log Cabin Camp:
Mrs. Rae Knighton, 53, 5800 Meadow Lake Rd., New Hope, a housewife.
Jens Gottlieb, an 80-year-old, 2727 N.E. Lincoln St., father of Mrs. Knighton.
Harry Long, about 65, 1029 Stryker Ave., West St. Paul.
Mrs. Long, 67.
At Bethany Fellowship camp:
Mrs. Edith Dugan, 62, 6820 Auto Club Rd., Bloomington. There are residences at the location.
Mrs. Harold E. Carlson, in her 50-es, wife of a livestock farmer at the fellowship.
The Rev. Arthur S. Olson, in his 70s, 7021 Augsburg Ave.

Family survivors recount tragedy

Rebecca Dugan   Edith Dugan

Cooler

The Minneapolis Tribune   THURSDAY

MINNEAPOLIS, MINN., THURSDAY, AUGUST 7, 1969   10c

Tornadoes Kill 14 in Northern Part of State

Outing Hit Hardest; Scores Are Injured

DALE CARLSON, 17, BLOOMINGTON

MINNESOTA

TWIN CITIES

TORNADOES HIT NORTHERN RESORT AREA

...ES BY ONE VOTE

jects 2 Attempts

M's Deployment

Moon Dust Has

'There Ain't Anything Anymore'

Outing Reports: 'God, It's Awful'

THE BRAINERD DAILY DISPATCH

"CENTRAL MINNESOTA'S DAILY NEWSPAPER"

BRAINERD, MINNESOTA 56401   SATURDAY, AUGUST 9, 1969   10 CENTS   VOL. 30, NO. 5

In place in the court of honor at the Crow Wing County Fair flower show which is taking the flower display is one of the top features of the fair each year. (Dispatch Photo)

Diver Finds Bodies
Of Two Children
In Roosevelt Lake

DRAGGING OPERATIONS—The bottom of the bodies of Roosevelt Lake near Brainerd, were recovered...

TERRY DUGAN AT HOSPITAL IN CROSBY, MINN.
Survived tornado that hit Lake Roosevelt

Youth Recalls His
Mother's Death

By DICK YOUNGBLOOD
Minneapolis Tribune Staff Writer

OUTING, Minn.—Young ... , 17, son of Brainerd,
Terry Dugan climbed to ... down for all at Roosevelt...

xon Asks Basic Income
r All Poor Families

nauts May Leave
antine Day Early

St. Paul Pioneer Press
First Newspaper in Minnesota

ST. PAUL, MINN., FRIDAY, AUGUST 8, 1969   30 PAGES   10 CENTS

121st YEAR—NO. 102

Sunday in the Women's Section

Back-to-School Fashions

What will the school site be wearing this coming term? Fashion writer Georgene Reelfis brings you the word in a colorful feature this Sunday.

Weather Takes
Peaceful Turn

Tax Reform
Bill Passed
By 394-30

Tax Reductions Of $9 Billion Included in Bill

WASHINGTON (UPI)

2 Still Missing in Tornado

13 Known Dead
In Resort Areas

By JACKIE GERMANN
Staff Writer

Outing Area Tornado Voted Top State Story

MINNEAPOLIS (AP)—A series of tornadoes which scarred northern Minnesota's majestic pine country, killed 15 persons and injured many more has been voted the top news story in the state for 1969.

Hardest hit in the Aug. 6 twisters was the Outing area about 150 miles north of the Twin Cities, where 12 died. The storms claimed more lives while cutting a mile path of death and destruction to the northeast.

Although it was the fifth time in five years that tornadoes hit the state death toll was the highest years.

Two stories vied for the No. 2 spot in the balloting by Associated Press writers.

Ranked second was the surprise resignation of James P. Shannon as auxiliary bishop of the St. Paul-Minneapolis Roman Catholic Archdiocese.

...was a strong third. Stenvig, stressing law and order, led the field in the primary, then swamped Republican Dan Cohen in the general election.

Two sports stories made...

the third on a misdemeanor charge.

The No. 6 story was probably No. 1 for southwestern and west-central Minnesota...

...lands and high water forces residents of low-lying areas to flee homes.

—Vikings roll up 12 straight victories and repeat as Central Division champions in National Football League.

St. Paul Dispatch

SECOND SECTION   FRIDAY, AUGUST 8, 1969   SEVENTEEN

CHAPTER 13

Things Don't Matter

Dick's brand new side-paneled blue station wagon lay underwater, his musical instruments and years of sermon notes still inside.

The next day, Thursday, we received Red Cross boxes with emergency toiletry supplies. A few of us went to the Ben Franklin in town to buy shoes and some clothes, courtesy of the Red Cross. Sheila picked out yellow canvas tennis shoes. It felt odd to be treated so special in the midst of so much loss.

Some teenagers from the Emily church took a few of us kids out to eat at a local restaurant in Crosby that afternoon. Eating out was rare for my family so this seemed like a really special occasion. My brother Jon ordered a piece of lemon cream pie and ate it while the teenagers made small talk to be polite.

"Do you have brothers and sisters?" one of them asked Sheila.

"I have a brother, but I'm not too sure about my sister," Sheila said, picking at her food. Divers were still searching for the bodies of Sharon Dugan and Paul Brokke.

After eating, we piled into a car. At some point during the drive, Jon suddenly got very sick. The shock had hindered his capacity to retain food. The driver stopped the car and Jon threw up his lemon cream pie on the side of the road.

⊷

As soon as he could access a phone, Dick Dugan called his brother Pat, who was interning with his wife Nedra at a Christian & Missionary Alliance church in Lincoln, Nebraska.

"A tornado's hit us," Dick said the moment Pat picked up the phone. "Mom and Becky are gone, and we can't find Sharon."

Pat couldn't believe his ears. "You're kidding."

"Would I kid about that?" Dick replied in a stricken voice.

Pat arrived in Outing on Friday, and Dick brought Pat down to the lake to see the devastation and wait for the divers as they searched the lake. Dick's brand new side-paneled blue station wagon lay underwater, his musical instruments and years of sermon notes still inside.

"Pat," Dick mused as the brothers looked across the lake, "things don't matter."

⊷

Dan Brokke drove back up to Lake Roosevelt to assist in the cleanup on Thursday. When he arrived, he tried to find the spot where he and his dad had taken refuge outside the cabin. He couldn't find a single place that wasn't covered with heavy trees. The fact that he and his dad could have easily died as well struck him. But Paul was still missing.

He also drove along Highway 6 to measure the destruction of the storm. He found about one mile total of storm damage, with one-half mile of very twisted trees and severe damage—the center of the tornado.

⁓

On Friday, August 8, after two days of looking for the bodies of the kids, the Sheriff called a diver from Brainerd, Bill Matthies. Bill quickly found Dan's brother Paul in 12 feet of water, lying between half of a canoe and a trailer. His shoulder had multiple fractures, and it was unclear if he had been knocked unconscious even before hitting the water. The thirteen-year-old lay on his stomach as if he were sleeping.

Bill emerged with Sharon two hours later. He found her body in 40 feet of water under the branches of a large leafy oak tree. Underwater the tree weighed very little and he was able to lift it off of her and bring her to the surface. She lay curled in the diver's arms, eyes closed, a small bruise on her forehead.

My Uncle Dick, along with Pat, was on the shoreline waiting for her.

CHAPTER 14

Crosby Hospital

Seventeen Dugans and not one's a Catholic!
—HOSPITAL CHAPLAIN

---

athy Brokke and I had arrived at the Crosby Hospital early, before the chaos set in. Every available nurse and doctor had been called in to help. Cots lined the halls and filled the lobby as droves of injured people and their families began to arrive. Doctors wheeled Cathy into surgery to suture her bloody scalp, a deep eight-inch long cut. Since I didn't need emergency medical attention and not knowing what else to do, I asked the receptionist at the ER desk if I could borrow a dime to use the payphone and call home to Bloomington.

The switchboard operator at Bethany connected me to Lucille Hegre, the wife of Ted Hegre, Bethany's president. I told her we had been hit by a tornado and that everything on Bethany's lake property was gone, everything. She asked about the people, and I told her what I knew.

"Becky Dugan and Edith Dugan are dead; Paul Brokke and Sharon Dugan are missing. I don't know anything about the Carlsons," I said at the end of my report. Because Lucille was having trouble hearing me, I had to repeat myself more loudly, "Becky Dugan is dead!"

And then I was alone. No one else I knew had yet arrived at the hospital. Because of my many nail punctures and scratches, I asked someone for a tetanus shot… and then I sat down on the curb outside the emergency room and sobbed.

Priscilla and Shane arrived together in an ambulance, and doctors immediately whisked Priscilla to the delivery room. The hospital was so full that there was no other place to put her, even though she was not going into labor.

"Be careful with my mom," little Shane told the doctors as they wheeled him into surgery, "She's going to have a baby." The gash in his forehead was so deep that he required many stitches, and the whites of his eyes had turned blood red from the trauma. But he was awake—and alive.

A Catholic priest came into Priscilla and Shane's hospital room to offer words of consolation, but all he could say was, "That's a hell of a thing to happen!"

As more of my family arrived at the hospital he commented, "I don't know how we'll ever recover. Seventeen Dugans and not one's a Catholic!" These remarks brought a bit of comic relief to my family in the coming days.

Doctors put Diane in the same room as Priscilla for the night. Other than a deep scrape on her back, a bump on her arm, and temporarily losing a contact lens—which ended up still being in her eye—Diane had emerged physically unscathed. The shock was another matter, however. Diane had no idea how she'd arrived at the hospital.

༝

Pastor Ezra Budke, a friend of Dick Dugan, had been vacationing in another part of Outing that week. He and his wife got back in town and had pulled into a gas station when suddenly the wind lifted their car up and set it back down. They knew something significant had occurred and drove to the Bethany property to see what had happened and were shocked to discover a tornado had hit the property.

He offered to take Terry, Dale, Ron, and Don—all with minor wounds—to the Crosby Hospital. Pastor Budke drove like a maniac pushing 100 miles per hour and insisting on passing as many cars as possible. Terry and Dale exchanged worried glances in the back seat.

"We're actually feeling pretty good!" Terry told Ezra as they sped past rows of downed trees, "We're fine! There's no hurry." *We've survived a tornado but we're going to get killed on this road*, Dale thought.

Doctors placed the boys in the same room where Terry's cuts on his neck and chin were sutured. His hurt arm was only bruised, not broken. The doctor who sewed the small gash above Dale's eyebrow seemed a little inebriated, shaking as he inserted the seven stitches. Dale tried to keep his composure and was certainly pleased when the final result looked normal.

A *Minneapolis Tribune* reporter came to the hospital on Thursday to interview the boys and take their pictures; the story appeared in the paper the next day. Reporters from the local

city paper, *Bloomington Sun*, also interviewed Dale. They demon
strated little emotion, as though these interviews were simply
business as usual.

↜

Friends and relatives who heard what had happened arrived
to help those who survived. Dan Brokke's uncle drove the three
hours from Minneapolis that evening and took Dan and Harold
to the hospital to see Cathy around 10:30 p.m. They visited with
Cathy and then returned home to Bloomington. When Dan finally
crawled into his own bed, exhausted and numb, he opened the
Scripture devotional on his desk to the reading for August 6. He
soon fell asleep with the comforting sense that God was in control.

↜

Reverend Jim Slye, the pastor of the Emily Wesleyan Methodist
Church, had conducted an afternoon service at a nursing home
that day in Deerwood, Minnesota, and on his return home around
4:00 p.m., drove by Serpent Lake between Deerwood and Crosby. He noticed the waves on the lake bouncing in the air rather
than rolling into shore and mentioned the unusual sight to his wife
Olive when he arrived home.

The parsonage stood right across the street from the church
on Highway 6. Jim and Olive stepped into their back yard and
heard a rumble. It sounded like a train and they tried to figure out
which train track the sound would be coming from. Interestingly,
there were no train tracks close by.

Sirens filled the air as ambulances and police cars sped north
past their home to Outing. Soon after, an ambulance headed south
to the hospital, and Jim decided to follow and see what was going
on. Dozens of people were milling around in the hospital hallways,

and he spoke with a few of them, including members of my family. Terry Dugan, Dale Carlson, Cathy Brokke, Diane Dugan, Priscilla Dugan, and Shane Dugan stayed at the hospital overnight so the doctors could monitor their wounds. Those of us not hospitalized needed a place to stay that night, and Pastor Jim and Olive welcomed us into their home, giving up their beds for us. When we arrived they prepared food for all of us. Jim soaked my feet in a pan of soapy water and looked for pieces of glass in my puncture wounds.

After dinner, we gathered in their living room, prayed, and sang the old hymn "I'd Rather Have Jesus Than Anything." We were all in shock and suffering from the unthinkable trauma we had survived. Four people we knew had died and three were still missing: five-year-old Sharon, thirteen-year-old Paul, and Rev. Arthur Olson. For my brother, Jon, somehow singing made sense of the chaos.

Jim said that the night before, Arthur and Minnie Olson and the Carlsons had attended a mission's prayer meeting with him and Olive at the home of church members who lived on Blue Lake. He never would have guessed their goodbyes would be the last.

My family slept in the pastor's bedroom, with Lon, Jon, and me sleeping on the floor. In the darkness, I heard my dad sobbing and my mom comforting him. He had lost both his mother and oldest child that day. It was just too much to take in.

My Uncle Dick didn't sleep that night either. He sat unmoving at the dining room table and finally broke down sobbing—it was three o'clock in the morning.

"I could stand it if I knew Sharon was dead," Dick said to Jim, who had stayed awake with him. "But thinking that she might be out there pinned underneath a tree and calling for Daddy...it's unbearable."

CHAPTER 15

The Funeral

Seven caskets, seven hearses, one thousand people.

I don't remember how I got home to Bloomington, or who I rode with. Most of the other survivors said the same thing. The shock had settled in by then, blotting out some memories and failing to register others. Don and Diane vaguely remember being in a station wagon with me.

Once the bodies of Paul and Sharon were found, a funeral was planned for that Monday at Bethany Missionary Church in Bloomington. A funeral home from Walker, Minnesota, brought the bodies back to Minneapolis after the death certificates had been registered.

We survivors had our first meal back at the Bethany campus in one of the smaller dining rooms. They served us by ourselves rather than having us mix with the other staff and campus residents. Diane felt like an alien sitting in the dining room—the entire situation seemed surreal. Jon felt an overwhelming sense of awkwardness seeing the other staff kids later that day. The kids had no idea what to say but wanted to help. "Here…here's underwear, Jon," one of them said, handing my brother a bag.

A diver had found Priscilla's purse in the lake with $300 cash inside. When they returned to Bethany to stay until after the funeral, they paper-clipped all the bills to a line they had strung up, and with the help of a few fans, dried them out. Daughter Sheila hated the smell of the wet, moldy paper, and couldn't tolerate being in the room.

The visitation was set for Sunday afternoon at Albin Funeral Chapel in Minneapolis, where the seven caskets were lined up in a couple of rooms. Evy Carlson and Minnie Olson's caskets stayed closed due to their severe injuries. Hundreds of people walked through the funeral home, and we stood next to our family members' caskets in a daze. Diane stood by her brother Pat and almost collapsed when she saw her mom.

The next day was the funeral at Bethany Missionary Church. Seven caskets, seven hearses, one thousand people. My family sat near the front on the left side of the church. The service was likely planned with little input from our families and lacked personal stories and remembrances. We were all still in shock. The processional to the Bloomington Cemetery after the funeral was the longest in Bloomington's history.

Two reactions to the tragedy at the funeral stuck with my dad, Toby. Someone came up to him, no doubt well-intentioned, and said, "It's good that you had four kids." Someone else mentioned how fortunate it was that Bethany's president hadn't been at the

Storm Tragedy Called 'Triumph' In Mass Funeral

From Death Unto Life

"Nay, in all these things we are more than conquerors through him that loved us. For I am persuaded, that neither death, nor life, nor angels, nor principalities, nor powers, nor things present, nor things to come, nor height, nor depth, nor any other creature, shall be able to separate us from the love of God, which is in Christ Jesus our Lord." — The Apostle Paul

(Taken from the program for the Bethany Missionary Church memorial service Monday)

Tornado Victim Tells of Terror, Initial Reactions

By FRANCES W. BERNS

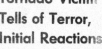

BLOOMINGTON SUN

Vol. 24, No. 33   TWO SECTIONS   Thursday, August 14, 1969   Second Class Postage Paid At Minneapolis, Minn.   20c

"For many Aug. 6 will be a day never to be forgotten," said Pastor T. A. Hegre, Bethany Missionary Church, 6820 Auto Club Road, Bloomington, as he spoke during memorial for seven Richfield and Bloomington tornado victims.

"For some that was a day of instant promotion from this life. For some it was a day they saw everything destroyed, but their lives spared."

"We read in the newspapers the tornado was a tragedy. In a sense it was, but we wonder if it should instead be called a triumph. Those who died have entered into the church triumphant," Pastor Hegre told the more than 1,000 persons who attended the funeral services.

Of those seated in the packed church, 200 were relatives of the seven deceased.

"Almost without warning the tornado struck. Three from Bethany remained in a cabin and the rest went into the lake. All were in the cabin but Harold and Dan Brokke who were outside.

"But those inside this house were taken up in this house by the tornado which had also ruined the water 40 feet high, and was smashed into this wall of water.

THE WATER ALSO released those who were in the house, or there would have been no hope for any of them."

It was only through a series of miracles that any of them escaped, Pastor Hegre said.

"Those who escaped should consider themselves living on borrowed time or as those living a resurrected life as having been brought back from death," Pastor Hegre told them of Bethany Fellowship who were spared by the tornado.

Speaking of the Rev. Arthur S. Olson, 46, and his wife, Minnie, 79, Pastor Hegre said, "The Olsons were missionary statesmen. They were numbered among the great.

"AND THEIR DAUGHTER, Evelyn, three of whose children have already completed missionary training here and two more with their training to complete." He was referring to Evelyn A. Carlson, 30, who taught English at the Bethany Missionary Training Center.

"And the Dugans, including the grandmother who raised her children for God," Pastor said, referring to Mrs. Edith A. Dugan, 62, a staff member of Bethany Fellowship who based this world on hers, but who now has entered into that place that is hers.

Becky was the 19 year old mentally retarded grandchild of Mrs. Dugan.

"And little Sharon Dugan and Paul Brokke. What a wonderful day in the Kingdom of Heaven."

WE MAY ASK why did it happen to these dear people," he said. "Can you think of any better people for it to happen to than these people who were ready to step into eternity?

"Some of these things happen to us because God loves us."

Also taking part in the ser-

FUNERAL
To Page 12

MOURNERS PACKED BETHANY MISSION CHURCH
Clergymen and pallbearers form procession following services

Storm Kills, Injures Bloomingtonites

A tornado roaring across Roosevelt Lake Aug. 6 left death, destruction and injury in its wake when it struck the four cabins belonging to Bethany Fellowship.

When the tornado passed on its way seven were dead and 12 were injured in the Bethany family camp.

IT WAS A FAMILY vacation for the families of Mr. and Mrs. Harold Carlson of Bethany, for Mrs. Carlson's aged parents Rev. and Mrs. Arthur Olson of Richfield, for Mrs. Edith Dugan of Bethany, her children and the families of her four married sons.

Also on vacation were the Harold Brokke family of Bethany.

It was 5 p.m. when the tornado struck.

At the time Mrs. Evelyn Carlson, 30, and her parents, Rev. and Mrs. Arthur Olson, 46 and 79, were in one of the two cabins built on the hill above the lake. The two

women were crushed to death by the force of the tornado. Rev. Olson was carried into the lake.

ALL OF THE OTHER dead and injured were in one of the two cabins built on a point on the bluff above the lake.

Rev. Olson   Mrs. Olson

lake. The cabin was picked up by the tornado and dashed into a 40 foot wall of water that was raised up from the lake.

The four who died in the cabin were Mrs. Edith Dugan, 62, Rebecca Dugan, 19, Sharon

Rebecca Dugan

Mrs. Edith Dugan

Mrs. Harold Carlson

Paul Brokke

Dugan, 5, and Paul Brokke, 13.

The bodies of Sharon and Paul were not recovered from the lake until Friday.

Hospitalized for treatment of their injuries were Mrs. Katherine Brokke, 42, Mrs. Priscilla Dugan, 33, and Sharo Dugan, 8.

Others who were treated and kept overnight in the hospital and released after treatment were Kenneth Dugan; Dianne Dugan, 20; Terry Dugan, 17; Susan Dugan, 17 the Rev. Richard Dugan; Dale Carlson, 17; Patrick Dugan, Ronald Dugan, and Mrs. Ronald Dugan.

parents and four other Bethany Fellowship members.

DALE'S FOREHEAD was still swollen from a blow he received during the tornado and the seven black silk stitches, closing two facial wounds, still were in place near his right eye.

"The first I knew of the tornado was when Harold Brokke came running into the cabin on the point where we all were. He said a tornado was coming and I looked out the window and saw it hit the Sieman's resort across the lake. It came right across the lake.

"It sounded like 100 trains. We were carried out through the air out over the lake and thrown into the water.

"The whole thing went so fast, I ended up in four feet of water and saw light over my head and came up for air. Then I went down again and came up the second time to stay.

"THE FIRST GUY I saw was Terry, (Terry Dugan, 17). I didn't think anybody would be alive. I don't know how we made it. I saw Terry and told him to hang on. Then I saw Shane (5-year-old Shane Dugan). Priscilla (Mrs. Richard Dugan, Shane's mother) and Sue Dugan. We told them all to hang on. I was about 15 feet from shore.

"Terry and I crawled out of the water first and then we helped Shane out. He had the worst head cut I have ever seen. I took off my shirt and wrapped it around his head. Terry's arm was cut and I tore off one of my pants legs and made a kind of sling for his arm.

"I used the other pants leg on my own head which was bleeding.

"I clearly remember every little detail of what happened. The first time I came up out of the water I noticed Dick Dugan's car parked in front of Cabin 3 and the second time I came up it was 150 yards down the shore right by me."

DALE RECALLED that he got one cut by his eye as he was flying through the air. The second time he came up he was hit in the head by a board.

"When we came out of the water there wasn't anything left on the hill and we didn't know where we were."

Dale explained that the cabin he had been in and the one the Brokke's had occupied before the tornado were located on a point on Lake Roosevelt. The other two cabins owned by Bethany Fellowship and used by staff members for family vacations were located up the hill.

WITNESS
To Page 12

STORM
To Page 12

RADIO
To Page 12

Suburban Volunteers Radio Storm Victims

By MICKEY TIBBITS

Around 1,000 messages were handled by amateur radio operators in Dr. Felton Jenkins' home, 8221 Morgan Ave.

"USUALLY WHEN an emergency strikes, telephone lines are down, or the system is swamped with calls coming

from all parts of the country, and a radio network is necessary to carry on emergency work," Dr. Jenkins explained.

The amateur radio operators worked in shifts for 54 hours after the tornado struck to handle communications between the twin cities and Out-

state and as far as into the lake. The cabin was picked up by the

Cross volunteers and medical came into the scene of the disaster.

They also made a list of the dead and injured and called the local radio stations asking them to tell people to stay off the roads, so that volunteers could get into the area.

DR. JENKINS' radio crew received messages from

every Red Cross station across the country from people who had friends and relatives in the area and others inquiring about property damage.

"We received a call from a woman in Birmingham, Ala.

SEVEN HEARSES WERE LINED UP IN FRONT OF BETHANY MISSIONARY CHURCH
Waiting for the Bodies of the Tornado Victims

ORDER OF SERVICE

Prelude

Invocation

Hymn / In Heavenly Love Abiding

Reading of the Scriptures

Prayer

Choir

Obituaries

Message from the Scriptures
Rev. Harald Grindal
Oak Grove Lutheran Church

Tribute
Rev. Lester A. Dahlen
American Lutheran Church—
Division of World Missions

Choir

Meditation
Rev. T. A. Hegre

Prayer

Benediction

Postlude

The funeral procession will form heading east on Auto Club Road. Interment services will be held first in Bloomington Cemetery, after which everyone is requested to return immediately to his car. The second procession will then form for those who wish to attend the interment at Sunset Memorial Park.

IN HEAVENLY LOVE ABIDING

In heavenly love abiding,
No change my heart shall fear;
And safe is such confiding,
For nothing changes here:
The storm may roar without me,
My heart may low be laid;
But God is round about me,
And can I be dismayed?

Wherever He may guide me,
No want shall turn me back;
My Shepherd is beside me,
And nothing can I lack:
His wisdom ever waketh;
His sight is never dim,
He knows the way He taketh,
And I will walk with Him.

Green pastures are before me,
Which yet I have not seen;
Bright skies will soon be o'er me,
Where darkest clouds have been:
My hope I cannot measure;
My path to life is free;
My Saviour has my treasure,
And He will walk with me. Amen.

FROM DEATH UNTO LIFE

"Nay, in all these things we are more than conquerors through him that loved us. For I am persuaded, that neither death, nor life, nor angels, nor principalities, nor powers, nor things present, nor things to come, nor height, nor depth, nor any other creature, shall be able to separate us from the love of God, which is in Christ Jesus our Lord."

—The Apostle Paul

BETHANY MISSIONARY CHURCH
August 11, 1969

This service held in loving memory of . . .

Paul Nathan Brokke

Age 13, of Bethany Fellowship, 6820 Auto Club Road. Survived by parents, Rev. and Mrs. Harold J. Brokke; brother, Daniel H., Bethany Fellowship; grandparents, Mr. and Mrs. E. J. Eliason, Bloomington, Mr. Halvor Brokke, Minneapolis. Interment Bloomington Cemetery.

Rebecca Louise Dugan

Age 19, of Bethany Fellowship, 6820 Auto Club Road. Survived by parents, Rev. and Mrs. LeRoy C. Dugan; sister, Suzanne Priscilla; 2 brothers, Lon and Jon, all of Bethany Fellowship; grandparents, Mr. and Mrs. Maurice L. Derscheid, Kenyon, Minnesota. Interment Bloomington Cemetery.

Mrs. Evelyn A. Carlson

Age 50, of Bethany Fellowship, 6820 Auto Club Road. Survived by husband, Harold; daughter, Mrs. David (Darlene) Anthony; 4 sons, Daniel, David, Darrell and Dale, all of Bethany Fellowship; 2 brothers, Rev. Albert S. Olson, Amery, Wisconsin, Orville A. Olson, Hibbing, Minnesota. Interment Sunset Memorial Park.

Sharon Lee Dugan

Age 5, of Huron, South Dakota. Survived by parents, Rev. and Mrs. Richard Dugan; sister, Sheila; brother, Shane, Huron; grandparents, Robert Newton and Mrs. Dorothy Newton, California. Interment Bloomington Cemetery

Mrs. Edith A. Dugan

Age 62, of Bethany Fellowship, 6820 Auto Club Road. Survived by 2 daughters, Mrs. Les (Norma) Westenberg, Rochester, Minnesota, Miss Dianne Dugan, Bethany Fellowship; 5 sons, the Rev. LeRoy C., Bethany Fellowship, Kenneth V., Canoga Park, California, the Rev. Richard, Huron, South Dakota, Patrick V., Lincoln, Nebraska, Terry, Bethany Fellowship; 9 grandchildren; 4 sisters, Mrs. Walter (Emma) Skeoch, Hawaii, Miss Marie Kriesel, Milwaukee, Mrs. Arthur (Ella) Neuleib, Owatonna, Mrs. Helen Smith, Los Angeles; 3 brothers, Fred and Albert Kriesel, Trempelau, Wisconsin, Ernest Kriesel, Owatonna. Interment Bloomington Cemetery.

Rev. Arthur S. and Minnie I. Olson

Age 80 and 79 respectively, of 7021 Augsburg Avenue, Richfield. Survived by 2 sons, Rev. Albert S., Amery, Wisconsin, Orville A., Hibbing, Minnesota; 9 grandchildren. Rev. Olson also survived by sister, Miss Luella Olson, Minneapolis, Mrs. Olson also survived by 5 sisters, Mrs. William (Ida) Lockren, Austin, Minnesota, Miss Olive Shirley, Miss Hilda Shirley and Mrs. Boyer (Esther) Egge of St. Louis Park, Miss Mabel Shirley of Northfield, Minnesota; brother, William R. Shirley, Minneapolis. Interment Sunset Memorial Park. (The Olson Family will return to Oak Grove Lutheran Church following the interment Service to meet Family and Friends.)

cabins that week, as though the rest of us were expendable. Such well-meaning comments often come to the grieving from others who simply don't know what to say.

The day was immensely difficult for all of us, but Darrell Carlson probably suffered the most. He attended his mother and grandparents' funeral, his girlfriend broke up with him, and he received his draft papers in the mail that would eventually send him to Vietnam.

One small positive involved two wallets he had left on the dresser in the upper cabin at the lake where his family stayed. Someone recovered the first one 50 miles away in one direction and the second 20 miles away in the other.

Jon stayed with a church family at some point during that first week, the Krauses, who took him out to eat at a restaurant for a cheese-stuffed hamburger. Jon felt conflicted about whether he should enjoy the experience—he was supposed to be sad because people had died, but everyone was treating him so nicely. Some-one gave a monetary gift to the survivors to replace items lost in the tornado, and Jon got $25—a king's ransom. It was his first time having disposable income. He remembers buying four large bot-tles of pop for a dollar at a nearby store.

We finished our two-week vacation after the funeral by visit-ing Owatonna, my dad's hometown. In the afternoon, we stopped to go swimming in a gravel-pit-turned-swimming hole, a familiar place from my dad's childhood. I jumped in and felt strangely in-vincible.

Diane was overwhelmed by grief at the unbearable loss of her mother. Alone one afternoon, she cried out to God for help and instantly felt a heavy weight lift off her shoulders. It was at that moment she knew she could go on. That was the first time she'd ever experienced God's presence in such a profound way.

Diane and Terry went home with their brother Dick and his family to Huron, South Dakota for a time. Diane wanted to get away—it just didn't feel right to be at Bethany without her mom. Terry returned to Bethany a few weeks later, but Diane decided to stay a while longer in Huron. The loneliness of being without her younger brother soon made her regret that decision.

One day, Diane and Priscilla were walking in downtown Huron when a strong gust of wind whipped around a street corner, slamming them in the face. Suddenly, Diane flashbacked to the utility cord that had wrapped itself around her neck while thrashing around in the lake. Instinctively, she tried to wrench it off, but nothing was there.

CHAPTER 16

Grief and Regrets

Forty years later I grieved. I guess there is no timeline or deadline for that.

---

don't think I ever really grieved after the tornado. As a seventeen-year-old who had just survived an unbelievable near-death experience, I don't think I processed the grief normally.

There were probably three reasons for this.

First of all, I had survived. There is a certain euphoria that goes with surviving what you were sure was going to kill you.

Secondly, I was in a state of shock even though I didn't realize it. Thinking back fifty years later, I realize there is a lot of that day that I just don't remember. Certain events are burned in my mind, but so much of the day and night are just gone.

And thirdly, the funeral was not conducive to grieving. The

last two bodies had been recovered on Friday, and then the funeral was scheduled for that Monday. Attending a seven-casket funeral where little time was spent talking about each of the individuals who had died rang hollow. The service was not personal to me.

About ten years ago, I took a virtual trip down memory lane. Our family had lived in Los Angeles for two years while my dad worked as a traveling evangelist. My mentally handicapped sister Becky and I walked two miles to school each day. From a very young age, I had taken on the role of the older sister. I soon passed her up in height and weight and translated her words since she had a speech impediment from hearing problems. She looked up to me, admired me, and loved me. I looked out for her but always felt a slight embarrassment. Selfishly I could talk her into loaning me money from her allowance if it suited my plans. All these memories surfaced from deep inside.

After my husband was long asleep, I used Google Earth to follow the route from our house in Los Angeles to the school where I attended sixth grade, and then further down the street to the junior high where I attended seventh grade. The buildings and houses we had walked by twice a day for two years brought back so many memories.

It was very late when I crawled into bed. Then unexpectedly, an overwhelming grief suddenly washed over me. For the first time, I was remembering my sister, our shared childhood, her vulnerabilities, and her love and devotion to me. For years I had hardly thought about her or missed her. And I had never cried for her, never. That night I lay in bed sobbing, trying not to wake my husband.

Forty years later I grieved.

I guess there is no timeline or deadline for that.

Over the past year, I started hearing from eyewitnesses and other survivors who shared their stories and memories with me. So many of them started their emails or phone calls by offering condolences and sympathy for what our family had endured. At first I thought, *That's really not necessary. It's been fifty years; I think I'm over it.* I found it odd that people treated the event like something that had just happened.

The reality is that I have cried more in these past two years of research and story gathering than ever before. The memories that have been reignited or learned about for the first time bring great emotion with them. I hope they have for the other survivors. It has been therapeutic.

We were very good at compartmentalizing our lives post-tornado. It is how we continued on with our lives without crumbling. We were unaware of anything like post-traumatic shock, but I am certain we all experienced it. We didn't go through any grief counseling, and people didn't want to talk about the event so as not to bring up the pain.

The Carlson boys, Darrell and Dale, lost their dear mom and both grandparents, and my friend Dan Brokke had lost his only brother, but I don't remember ever offering them sympathy or condolences. I should have.

Life took on a new normal. We held the hurt and sadness inside of us for many, many years.

CHAPTER 17

Life Goes On

My dad spent many weeks angry at God
because of Becky's death.

erry and I started Bible school at Bethany College of Missions (now Bethany Global University) that September. Other than Diane becoming my roommate, life sort of returned to normal.

We hardly ever talked about the storm other than the occasional reference. We shared no details of our experiences with each other. Once in a while, my mom mentioned how she heard Becky's call for help, saw her struggling in the water, and couldn't get to her because she couldn't swim. I heard the pain in her voice, but I never asked for any more details—I didn't want to relive any painful memories. I wish now that I had; it would have been healing for both of us. I know that memory haunted her, but my mom was by nature very emotionally steady. She seemed to cope better than my dad.

My dad and my Uncle Dick had both lost their mom and a daughter within minutes, and their grief was overwhelming. Both were ordained ministers, both in full-time Christian service. Why had this tragedy happened to their families?

My dad spent many weeks angry at God because of Becky's death and would go for walks, feeling guilty for being away from the cabins when the tornado blew through. Though his guilt was irrational, he felt it deeply. He would have been powerless against the winds just like the rest of us. If anything, he saved Jon, Lon, and Sheila's lives by insisting they come with him to the hardware store in Emily.

On one of those walks, he again asked God, "Why did you allow Becky to die?"

My dad said he heard God say in an almost audible voice, "You were so worried about Becky and were praying for me to take care of her. She's with me now, so why are you mad at me?"

It's true, my parents had been wondering about Becky's future. She had graduated from the State School in Owatonna and had been working at Opportunity Workshop (now named Opportunity Partners), a learning and job-training center for people with disabilities. As with all parents of handicapped children, questions about her future loomed large, and they were asking God to take care of Becky. God's reply was what my dad needed to hear.

My Uncle Dick also wrestled with the question of why God had taken his daughter. In his anguish, he said to God, almost in defiance, "You gave your Son, and I've given my child, too." In response, he felt God say, "But I gave mine willingly." In a strange way, perhaps, this comforted him. God understands our grief.

⬅

Dale Carlson ended up missing the first week of high school football practice his senior year at Lincoln High School in Bloomington. When his coach came up to him on the field and chastised
him for being late, Dale explained that his mother, grandparents,
and other close friends had died in a tornado. The coach replied,
"I'm sorry to hear that, but it's time to put that behind you and play
football."

Dale had never experienced such a heartless response. He
graduated from high school a year after Terry and me and initially
planned on attending college on an ice hockey scholarship. After
the tornado, he changed his plans and decided to attend Bethany
College of Missions instead.

CHAPTER 18

Survivor's Guilt

You asked about survivor's remorse.
I carried that for years.
—Shane Dugan

According to mental health professionals, people who survive life-threatening trauma while others lose their lives, often struggle with feelings of guilt. Why were their lives spared? Was there something they could have done to prevent the loss of life?

All but one of the survivors I talked to had the same reaction when I asked them about survivor's guilt, aptly summed up by my Aunt Priscilla, who exclaimed, "Gosh, what a stupid question!" She couldn't imagine that anyone would need to feel guilt.

"I'm just glad I know where people went," Priscilla said, "I don't know how people who aren't Christians survive things like this. We have such hope. I don't know how they do it."

"I remember feeling guilty about how quickly I wanted to get out of there," Terry said. "We did the minimum for Shane and I just didn't want to do any more. Over the years, I sometimes felt guilty about that, like I could have been a more selfless and heroic person than just wanting to run. I don't know if you could call it survivor's guilt."

But when it was Shane's turn to speak, he said, "You asked about survivor's remorse. I carried that for years."

"Why didn't you say something?" Priscilla asked her son, rather astonished.

"Because," Shane replied, "the day of the tornado you had told me, 'Keep an eye on your sister.'"

I don't suppose a six-year-old had words to describe his feelings at the time. But the lack of conversation about this through the years is just another example of how we all dealt with our pain—by silence. Even though Priscilla had lived with Shane and his family since Uncle Dick's death, the topic never seemed to surface.

CHAPTER 19

The Man in the Gray Shirt

And then I brought up the man who had seen
Sharon's body suspended over the bay.

The more I interviewed survivors and eyewitnesses, the more I discovered how incredibly miraculous this entire story was. One of these moments happened when I spoke with the diver that found Paul and Sharon's bodies.

The Brainerd Dispatch issue from August 9, 1969, stated that Paul and Sharon had been found by Bill Matthies, a diver from Brainerd, Minnesota. As I began gathering information for this book, I added him to my list of people to contact. I learned that Bill was a high school math teacher, and also the owner and founder of the Minnesota School of Diving and had been diving since the 1950s. He opened his dive shop in Brainerd in 1959, ten years before the Outing tornado.

However, Bill ended up contacting me first. I received an email from his son, Jim, the same day the article about my search for information was published in the *Brainerd Dispatch*. Bill had recovered 99 drowning victims in his diving career, but recovering Paul and Sharon had a significant impact on him. The kids reminded him of his own two children, a son and a daughter. The memories of their small, lifeless bodies haunted Bill for years, and nightmares woke him up to check on his own children for a long time after the recoveries.

Jim said that his dad wanted me to have a copy of his book about his diving career, *One Earth Two Worlds*, so I could leaf through the two chapters that mentioned the Outing tornado. I received the book in the mail two days later, a handwritten note from Bill tucked under the front cover. Curious, I opened the book.

"You won't believe this story!" I exclaimed as I read the following out loud to my husband Scott.

"I found the body of the young boy quickly but was having trouble finding the young girl. A man came up to me while I was changing air tanks on the shore and said he had some information he thought might be useful in locating the child. He told me that he could remember seeing the little girl suspended in the air over a certain section of the bay.

We were a little skeptical of his directions because this same man said he was also lifted by the storm, carried out over the lake, carried back over the land, and then carried back over the lake again and dropped in the water. It was during this ordeal that he had seen the little girl suspended in the air over the bay. We moved our search to the place he told us to look and it was there that I found the child."

This information didn't match anything I had from any of the other survivors. My uncles Kenny and Dick had died by the time I began my research and I was unable to interview them. No one else told a similar story.

My Aunt Priscilla, Sharon's mom, eagerly agreed to accompany me to visit Bill. We both wondered if the man that told Bill where Sharon was could have been an angel.

I said to Priscilla, "The Lord promised to go through the storm with us, didn't He? He would have wanted Sharon's body found."

We decided to accept the story as told, even though we would have preferred more clarification. I added "finding Sharon" to my list of questions for our upcoming visit with Bill.

In the meantime, Jim Matthies contacted Bill's diving tender, Gary Fitch, so he could meet with us also. In another email, Jim told me this:

"Gary helped my dad with many dives, but what he remembers most about this one is how Dad spent an unusually long time bringing Sharon up after he found her. Gary discovered later that he had spent extra time untangling her hair and wiping the dirt and mud off her. Dad didn't know who would be waiting in the pontoon and wanted to make sure that she looked okay."

It brought tears to my eyes. I couldn't wait to meet Bill and his son.

In July 2019, Priscilla, my daughter Shannon, my granddaughter Delia, and I drove from our cabin in Crosslake to meet Bill Matthies at his home in Brainerd. Priscilla gladly brought photos of Sharon at Bill's request. It was an emotional and interesting hour and a half, attended also by the *Brainerd Dispatch* publisher, Pete Mohs, and his photographer, Steve Kohls. We told our stories to the group and answered questions.

And then I had a chance to ask Bill questions. Where in the lake were the bodies found? How deep? What was the cause of death? Bill was quite sure they had both drowned because their bodies did not appear otherwise injured.

And then I brought up the man who had seen Sharon's body suspended over the bay. "No one has told me a story that's anything like that!" I said. Bill stood by the account as he had written it.

"Do you remember what the man looked like that talked to you?" I asked.

"Well," Bill said, "he was a little bit older, so he might not be around anymore. And he was wearing a gray shirt."

～

An addendum to the book *One Earth, Two Worlds* arrived from Bill Matthies in August of 2019. Part of the addendum read as follows:

> "After reading this story about Sharon, *The Song in Sharon's Purse: How a Loving God Prepared a Child for Heaven,* by Priscilla Dugan, it kept going through my mind that this story seemed deeply religious. I had Jim contact Pastor Hans from Trinity Lutheran Church here in Brainerd to get his opinion. He said that not every religious event can be explained. He said they are referred to as a *God Thing.*

This made perfect sense to me since it seemed like a *God Thing* to me.

I got thinking about another event in this story which I can't explain. Do you remember in the story that when I was changing tanks a man came up to me and explained that when he was picked up by the tornado and circled over the lake that he saw a little girl who was also picked up by the tornado and dropped in the lake? The thing that bothers me is how could anybody that is picked up by a tornado that is circling over the ground and the lake have enough stability to observe a little girl also circling over the lake and remember where she had landed, so he could tell me where to look, which pretty much guaranteed Sharon's recovery.

The thought occurred to me that he was possibly a messenger directed by a higher authority to keep track of Sharon and report her location to me, whether he knew what he was doing or not. By some strange coincidence, if this is true, I believe that I just witnessed another *God Thing*."

CHAPTER 20

Ready for Heaven

*For her parents, all of these stories pointed to a loving
God preparing a little girl for heaven.*

---

t has become increasingly evident to me that God prepares people for death. Here are some examples from the stories I was told.

Sharon Dugan

Dick and Priscilla Dugan had planned to have Sharon start kindergarten that fall in Huron, South Dakota where Dick pastored a church. Priscilla told Sharon they needed to go shopping for school clothes. Sharon calmly told her mother that she wouldn't be going to school.

"Everyone goes to school," Priscilla told her.

"I won't," Sharon responded.

Oh, boy, here we go, Priscilla thought, but she let the matter drop and decided to discuss it later.

The Sunday before the Dugans left for vacation, Sharon skipped around the church after the service, telling the adults and her friends goodbye and that she wouldn't see them again. The adults explained that she would be back after two weeks, but Sharon continued with her farewells.

"My mom is going to have a girl to take my place," Sharon told her Sunday School teacher, who explained that she would be a big sister, not replaced. (Sheri Lee Dugan was born October 20, 1969.)

One of the church nursery volunteers overheard her wondering aloud what Christmas would be like in heaven.

The congregation had been learning a new song in church and before the Dugans left for Minnesota, Sharon had tucked a copy into her little purse and packed it with her belongings.

The rescue divers found Sharon's purse in the lake among the debris, the song lyrics still inside:

> *In a little while, my Lord will come for me.*
> *In a little while, His blessed face I'll see.*
> *In a little while, when this life's race is run,*
> *I'll hear Him say to me,*
> *"My child, well done."* *

For her parents, all of these stories pointed to a loving God preparing a little girl for heaven.

⤙

Although unexplainable, years later, the Dugans' next-door neighbor, Abby, who was Sharon's age at the time, told Priscilla that Sharon had visited her every day from August to November after the tornado. Sharon would knock on the front door and the two girls

*From *In A Little While* ©Natalie Haig

would play together. When Abby's birthday came in November, a huge snowstorm swept through Huron. No one was able to come to her birthday party...except Sharon. As the girls sat playing on the living room rug, Abby looked at Sharon.

"You're not coming back anymore, are you?" she asked.

Sharon smiled. "No, I've got to go."

Abby never saw her again after that.

Becky Dugan

Becky knew that she was different from the people around her and she didn't like it. Her mental handicap bothered her. She was also hard of hearing from numerous ear infections as a child and wore a hearing aid. She had a speech impediment because of it, and I used to *translate* what she said when we were little because I could understand her. She loved to talk and was very outspoken about her opinions.

When I started dating, she felt left out—she was older than me, after all, and liked boys too. She had crushes on all the cute ones.

One evening, about a year before the tornado, our dad took Becky out on a father-daughter date to dinner and a movie. He knew she felt excluded and wanted her to feel special. She made a comment while they ate. "Daddy, I don't belong in this world," Becky said. I'm sure my dad tried to console her in some way, but Becky couldn't get the notion out of her head.

My brother Jon's dream about Becky's death the night before the tornado comforted my parents immediately afterward. It proved that God hadn't been asleep—He knew about it beforehand.

Edith Dugan

My grandmother was the only one of her nine siblings to graduate from high school. She then attended a year of normal school to become a teacher. She ran an organized house and was a great seamstress. She had a good sense of humor, sang alto, and had a knack for arts and crafts. None of us ever heard her complain.

Edith's love for the Lord and for others was overwhelmingly evident in everything she did. Despite her shy nature, Edith's commitment to Christ enabled her to reach out to others with the Gospel. She and my grandfather, Bernard, ran a rural Sunday school ministry near their home in Owatonna for several years. My grandma also held an after-school Good News Club in her home for children in the community.

After Bernard died in 1964 and she, Pat, Diane, and Terry moved into the Bethany dormitories, we all could tell she was very lonely and missed her husband terribly. None of us remember her talking about death before the tornado, but there is no doubt she welcomed heaven with arms stretched wide.

Evy Carlson

Evy was born in Honan, China, and lived there until she graduated from high school and then attended college in Minneapolis, Minnesota. She taught English at Bethany Bible College and made an authentic Chinese meal for the senior class every year. She loved the students, especially those who came from foreign countries, and was always available to lend a listening ear.

Evy's death was very grievous for her husband, Harold, but he never questioned God about why this tragedy happened. He recalled the many conversations with Evy over the previous months about the brevity of life and the need for the family to be ready to meet the Lord, and it was obvious to him that God knew all along what was going to happen.

Evy spoke of these things matter-of-factly. The topic seemed to come up often and although Harold agreed with her, it didn't dawn on him until after the tornado that God had been preparing Evy for her death. In turn, she was preparing her family also, by emphasizing the importance of being ready, as we never know how much time we have on earth. Recalling their conversations brought a quiet assurance to Harold that the Lord had been present through it all.

Rev. Arthur and Minnie Olson

Arthur and Minnie Olson were pioneer Lutheran missionaries to China for 49 years. The beloved couple had led many people to know the Lord throughout that time. When they returned to the United States and retired, they both developed pleurisy. After their deaths, the Carlson family learned that they had prayed "that the Lord would take them quickly and that He would take them together." Arthur and Minnie knew they would soon be with the Lord and were already headed in that direction.

Paul Brokke

Somehow, Paul had a sense that heaven was not far away for him. Starting about a month before the vacation, after playing baseball in the afternoons, Paul would come into the house and spend an hour studying the book of John on his own. Something had really touched the thirteen-year-old's heart that summer. He asked his mom a few weeks before the trip, "You and Dad and Dan are ready, aren't you?"

Cathy inquired, "Yes, why do you ask?"

"I just want to be sure we'll all be together."

After Paul was gone, the Brokkes found comfort in the reality that their family had an advance man in heaven waiting for them.

CHAPTER 21

Borrowed Time

Life is a fragile gift—we must not take it for granted.

We don't always get an answer to why things happen. Weather events take place constantly and tremendous suffering follows. Bad things do happen to good people and good things do happen to bad people. Life deals out experiences that are unexplainable to the natural mind and emotions.

Many of us cried out to God immediately after the tornado swept through, including myself. There is a sudden clarity that comes when you think you are dying—your own helplessness to save yourself, and your need for Someone stronger than the storm!

My immediate realization after the tornado was that life is a fragile gift—we must not take it for granted. I never really questioned why the event happened, but I know now more than ever that it's a miracle any of us lived to tell the story. Maybe we don't have as much time as we think. Death and eternity are truly just a breath away.

What I have come away with over the last two years is the realization that God was present in the midst of this storm. Looking back on all the stories that came to light, I see God's hand in so many ways. An outstanding example of this is when Cathy Brokke first surfaced after being thrown in the lake. She immediately feared for Paul. However, peace washed over her at that moment as though God were saying, "It's all right. It's part of my plan and purpose; trust me." She knew God wanted their family to love and trust Him even if their family never understood all the reasons for what had happened.

The way we deal with tragedy depends on our understanding of God. I don't believe God sent the tornado. By faith I believe, as the Apostle Paul states in Romans 8:28, that He can make all things work together for good even though I don't understand how or have all the answers.

I appreciate the opening words of Pastor Hegre's funeral sermon more today than I did fifty years ago and can now believe that out of great tragedy God can bring good.

> "For many, August 6 will be a day never to be forgotten. For some, it was a day of instant promotion from this life. For some, it was a day they saw everything destroyed, but their lives spared. We read in the newspapers that the tornado was a tragedy. In a sense it was, but we wonder if it should instead be called a 'triumph.' Those who died have entered into the church triumphant. It was only through a series of miracles that any

of them escaped. Those who escaped should consider themselves living on borrowed time or as those living a resurrected life as having been brought back from death." (Pastor T. A. Hegre, August 11, 1969)

I am a survivor. I am living on borrowed time.

Fifty Years Later
We Remembered

Fifty years ago today, the unthinkable happened.
And we are here to remember it.
—SUE DUGAN MOLINE

---

t was a hot, sunny Tuesday in Outing, Minnesota. The date was August 6, 2019, fifty years to the day from the horrific storm that changed so many lives. The Outing Area Chamber of Commerce had planned the event which included a Survivor's Picnic and program, and dedication of two granite benches commemorating the F4 tornado and its victims.

A flyer was distributed announcing the event called *Winds of Remembrance.* I did my part to advertise the picnic, inviting every family member I knew and sending the flyer to all those who called with their storm stories.

It was an amazing success. More than three hundred people gathered in the small town of Outing—the count based on how many hot dogs and bottles of water were served. Large boards were available to post pictures and posters and newspaper stories, and hundreds of people walked by.

Many survivors and their family members showed up to remember. Most of my children and grandchildren were there, along with aunts, uncles, and cousins. I met three other survivors for the first time—Nancy (Borris) Holscher, and Pam and Jeanna Marko, wonderful ladies who had carried their own memories and grief for many years. I met Denise Ramacier, whose grandparents Harry and Olga Long had been killed.

A local singer named Katie, a former *American Idol* contestant, beautifully sang "On Eagle's Wings" and "God Bless the U.S.A.", and the Fire Chief said a few words.

I had been asked to speak as part of the program. By this time my story and the story of the upcoming 50th Anniversary of the August 6th tornado had been printed in seven newspapers and aired on two TV stations—WCCO and KARE-11. I had been gathering stories and historical information for over a year.

I started by thanking the organizers of the event: the Outing Area Chamber of Commerce—Meri Lysne, LeAnn Werner, Jim Brown, and Mary Weihrauch. They had done an amazing job putting it together. (Sadly, Mary Weihrauch passed away suddenly on August 19, 2019, at age 46, two weeks after the event.)

My next words were filled with emotion: "Fifty years ago today, the unthinkable happened. And we are here to remember it. And it should be remembered." I went on to share my story and just a few of the stories from the more than 130 people I had heard from. Pat and Nedra Dugan sang "Whirlwind"—a song my Uncle

Pat had written about the tornado. Other survivors shared their memories and my Aunt Priscilla tearfully read her story, *The Song in Sharon's Purse.*

At 5:00 p.m. the church bells rang in remembrance and we took our families back to the site of the former Bethany Cabins on Sunset Hill Road. A beautiful family cabin, owned by friends of Bethany, now sits on the point, and the trees and lake are beautiful once again.

And our Dugan family talked and talked, shared stories, and remembered. It was so good for us.

Acknowledgments

As mentioned in my Dedication, this book is only possible because of the contributions of hundreds of people who shared their memories, stories, and pictures with me. Although it is a personal story, it is also a historical record of August 6, 1969, and the events surrounding that day. Special thanks are given to David Sluka, a friend in the publishing world, who encouraged me to write this story. He came up with ideas to keep the project moving forward and provided the accountability I needed to do so. A very special thank you is due to his daughter, Elizabeth Sluka, who took my extensive research and transcripts, combined them with my memories, and turned them into a story. She now credits herself as being the #2 expert on the Outing tornado. She was delightful to work with and is a very talented young lady.

I had three wonderful editors and proofreaders—my aunts Diane (Dugan) Dahlen and Nedra Dugan, and my writing coach Tammy Foster from Michigan. They each corrected, improved and polished the manuscript to make it ready for publishing. I cannot express enough appreciation to my uncle, Terry Dugan, who provided the incredible cover design and book design. He always helped me on short notice and his talent speaks for itself.

Two "up north" Minnesota newspapers provided the publicity that brought in stories and pictures from countless sources. Pete Mohs, publisher of the *Brainerd Dispatch*, and Paul Boblett, editor of the *Northland Press*, provided the invaluable visibility that compelled me to share these many stories in book form. Two local Minneapolis TV stations also shared the story—Jennifer Mayerle, reporter from WCCO-TV, and her cameraman, Aaron Goodyear, first covered the story in July of 2019, and KARE-11 reporter, Boyd Huppert, in August of 2019. This publicity yielded much new material and I thank you for that coverage.

Thanks to Deb Rose, a photographer with the Minnesota Department of Natural Resources. Within ten minutes of my call to the DNR, Deb Rose located six 50-year-old slides in a three-ring binder and scanned and emailed them to me the next day. These never-before-seen photographs are invaluable. I also want to thank my dear friends who acted as readers and honest critics— my cousin Ruth (Jolivette) Asper, Leslie Iverson, and Mary Little. Mary also accompanied me on information-gathering outings and provided me assistance in so many other ways.

Finally, thank you to my patient husband, Scott Moline, who put up with many hours of listening to me talking to strangers on the phone and reading emails from eyewitnesses. He was always available to bounce stories and ideas off of and encouraged me to complete this project. My four daughters, Shannon Tacheny, Erin Olson, Alison Webb, and Lauren Ashley Johnson encouraged me and provided their expertise and assistance in launching this book. They are the best daughters any mom could wish for and I love them dearly. My 13 grandchildren motivated me to write this story and leave them some family history. Mimi loves you Delia, Hunter, Tessa, Kensie, Kallista, Kora, Sawyer, Scarlett, Hazel, Stryker, Cruz, Jax and Jet! If I have forgotten to thank anyone, I apologize. I appreciate you tremendously.

Odds and Ends

I was fascinated by every little detail that I learned while research-
ing this story. Not all of them fit into the narrative of the book, but
I think they are all interesting and add to the historical value.

This Request for Information was printed in several northern
Minnesota newspapers. The phone started ringing and I received
emails daily, but I never did receive any photos of the actual tornado.

EYEWITNESSES WANTED to 1969 TORNADO

A survivor of the F4 tornado that hit Roosevelt Lake in
Outing, Minnesota, on August 6, 1969, is looking for
eyewitnesses to that event. This August marks the 50th
anniversary of that tornado that killed 7 of her family
members and friends at the Bethany Cabins on Roosevelt Lake, as well as many others. She would appreciate
any photos of the actual tornado or damage afterward,
or any eyewitness accounts or memories shared by family or community members. No detail remembered is
too small to share.

These are some of the responses:

Diana Thomas (now in her 90s)—her family had a cabin on the
south end of Roosevelt Lake since 1925. Her memory of that day:
"I can remember the hummingbird feeders would not stay filled."

Alice (Olds) Hawkinson—took the picture of her sister Margaret sitting on the rubble of the Long's house. She remembers a tree with an ironing board wrapped around it.

Dan Steiner from Crosby, Minnesota, was age 13—His uncle, Gary Steiner, was working on the roof of Outing Marine when the tornado hit. His uncles had chain saws so worked as loggers after the storm. His uncles told him about seeing fish in the woods, five miles from any lakes.

Divers in Roosevelt Lake—While working on recovery, they opened a refrigerator and found a carton of unbroken eggs. They opened the carton and the eggs started floating to the surface of the lake. From the book: *One Earth Two Worlds*.

George Carleton from Emily did search and rescue work at Simmons Resort. He saw a D-8 caterpillar that had been picked up and moved 20 feet. It did not roll—just moved.

Van Bialon from Emily was 22—"Early next morning we drove to Outing and saw the devastation…horrific. I very much remember walking along the shoreline noticing an impossible occurrence. I found about a 12" piece of straw which was forced by the power of the tornado into an 8" birch tree. The weird thing is that you could see daylight through the straw. It was like looking through a wide soda straw. It went 100% through the tree like a long hollow nail. I have never seen or heard of anything like it again ever."

Rodney Buckingham was younger that day but remembers it well—Years later "we made a scuba dive on the lake in 1993. There is stuff scattered all over the lake bottom. Everything you could imagine being in those cabins is down there. I was swimming along in about 30' of water when I found a pair of women's white high-heeled shoes just inches apart from each other.

I couldn't help but wonder how after all the flying around those shoes had gone through that they ended up next to each other."

Pat Maranda had just arrived in Vietnam in the summer of 1969. A neighbor from the Outing area mailed him newspapers about the tornado. He kept the newspapers for 50 years and handed them to me at the 50th Anniversary picnic. Very touching!

Vernon Chenevert from Remer—his family owned 160 acres east of Outing. Following the tornado, the forests had to be bulldozed and cleared, and then he planted 40,000 trees "with his own two hands" while his dad drove the tractor.

Anne Kletten was living in Norway when she read it in the paper there. She made a mental note because she was moving to Remer the following July. She later married Robert Burch of Remer, a game warden at the time of the tornado. He had spent days on end in the search and rescue efforts. She said it was a "nightmare that stayed with him for the rest of his life."

Denny Lee from Omaha, NE, was age 14 in the summer of 1969 and was spending the summer with his grandfather on Big Trout Lake near Crosslake. August 6 was a very hot and humid day with very little wind. Late in the afternoon, the color of the sky changed. Unlike anything Denny had ever seen, the sky became a combination of green, blue, and red. He just felt that something was brewing as the clouds became darker and threatening. He and his grandfather, intrigued by the change in the weather, went outside their cabin at Manhattan Beach to take a look. As Denny and his grandfather watched, they saw the tornado develop and move west to east over the treetops several miles north of their location. (Big Trout Lake is about 17 miles by road from Outing and 4 or 5 miles south-east of Stewart Lake.) They drove over to

Outing the next morning and observed horrific damage.

Glenda Fawkes Nyberg—"I was at our log cabin (built in 1927) on the northwest side of the north end of Roosevelt Lake. We left to find shelter and were on the bridge at Outing when a water-spout came from the south end. Our station wagon was pushed to the left side of the bridge, released and we continued to Crosby-Ironton. We were covered in sand, as was the interior of the car. My four young children and I felt very lucky."

Curtis Letch was age 5—"I vividly remember this as my family knew the owners of the Outing general store and had stopped to visit them. We were in the store when the tornado went through the park on the lake in Outing. I can still remember my mom yelling at my dad to go in the basement as he stayed upstairs to watch the tornado cross the lake. He claimed he saw the bottom of the lake."

Kay Wittgenstein and her good friend Jan were 19 that summer and were vacationing about six miles from Outing—"On the day of the tornado it was raining, so we decided to go into Outing just to look at stuff. As we were driving we noticed branches and things were down and we soon realized it was from a current storm. Soon it got worse with power lines down. As we were driving a gentleman came running up a hill from the lake yelling to go get help—that a resort had been flattened. We had no idea there were any buildings there as we couldn't see them. We went into Outing to get help. We were the first ones passing through from the resort. We were pretty shook up by the tragedy."

Dr. Jean Rock—"My Dad, Richard Albie, was the Ambulance Director for the Crosby Hospital at the time of the Outing torna-do. He and his partner, Walt Haag, were the first ambulance crew on the scene. He spent three straight days and nights in Outing, attempting to rescue those he could. My Mom didn't know where he was, except that it was bad. We would occasionally see the ambulance go by with lights and sirens on, and we'd look to try and see him. I was a young child at the time, and I remember his reflections—the stories about the people—and it bothered him, those he could not save. There were great stories of rescue with many volunteers helping, and also heartbreaking stories of loss."

Patti Muck Giese— "I was there that day, and my parents and I watched from the kitchen table of our one room cabin, which was just a few feet from the shore on the north end of Lake Roosevelt as the tornado passed through. I was 15 years old, and we had just returned from a driving vacation around the northland, and were stopping at the cabin for a night before heading back to Minneapolis. We had a clear view looking down the lake to the south. The thick gray cloud came over the trees and appeared to descend onto the lake from our vantage point. I remember my parents saying, 'Look that's a funnel cloud, right there,' and then they were silent. Driving through Outing (a day or two later), there was what appeared to be a body covered with a sheet under a tree. There were many responders and aid workers. I don't think we knew the scope of the tragedy at that time, but we knew it was bad. My mother said the level of the lake actually went down quite a ways."

Candace Lilyquist was a year and a half old when this happened but she listened to stories from her relatives for years—"For my entire childhood, every time we drove through Outing my parents said that there was a whole house with the table set for dinner in the lake. I pictured this with my child's brain and never go through Outing without thinking of it."

Rick Wigand and his friend Terry Bray drove up from the Twin Cities the weekend of August 8, 1969. Terry had a cabin on Mitchell Lake nearby. "We drove up and saw the devastation. His area had some damage but as we travelled toward Roosevelt, the path of the tornado was evident. About a mile wide swath had leveled everything. Trees looked like pick-up sticks and the damage in your area was a war zone—rescue vehicles everywhere and closed to traffic. Notable was the fact that Terry is allergic to bee stings and carried an injector at all times while up north. At his cabin that weekend none of the wasps and hornets which were deadly to him were to be seen—no birds either."

Susan Ashwood was eight years old and remembers that day as though it was just yesterday. "We were on Leavitt Lake at my great Uncle Orville and Great Aunt Olive's cabin, just spending a nice afternoon with them, nine of us in the cabin. I can remember hearing the roaring of the tornado as it came toward us. My Great Aunt Olive was in a wheelchair and we all got her into the bedroom with us. My Dad hid behind the refrigerator. I was sitting on the bed when it hit. The tornado came up off the lake onto us. The cabin we were in was found over a mile away from us. The only way out was by boat. I remember the outhouse was lifted up and placed back down on a bunch of trees but in the same spot. It is a storm that I will never forget."

Terry Berczyk was at Pelican Lake with his father and grandfather, moving boats further up on the beach before the storm hit. "We watched the storm move across the west side of Pelican Lake and move north. I remember seeing a large very black cloud and my grandfather saying he hoped nobody was in the path of that storm because it looked really bad. The following day or so, my father and I drove up to Outing. As we came around a corner after the bridge, there was a group of police and people gathered to the right on the shoreline. We realized they were removing a body from the water. I believe it was the missing five-year-old. My father told me to look away, but I was a curious ten-year-old. I will always remember that moment. It was a quiet drive home."

Randy Cray, age 12, was at the south end of Roosevelt with his grandmother, Kathleen Cray. "We went to the picture window looking west over the lake. We saw the tornado coming directly at us but when it got close to the lake it turned north. The next morning we drove to Emily to phone home as we did not have a cabin phone. The line at the pay phone was way over a block long."

Mary Jane Derscheid (Sue's aunt) "I just remember driving into the drive at Bethany and there were 7 funeral coaches lined up in front of the church. It just took my breath away."

Nancy Carlson (Mrs. David Carlson) "I was about to marry David Carlson and got the news that his mom and grandparents were taken in the tornado. On the way home from the funeral Harold (Carlson) broke out in song, 'How Great Thou Art'. My heart broke in two that moment as I saw in him such a faith and so much pain."

Dan Miller, Meteorologist with the National Weather Service-Duluth. Three of us survivors (Terry, Diane, and myself) met with Dan and Joseph Moore in June of 2019. Dan showed us a PowerPoint presentation about the tornado used in a recent conference. The presentation ended with this sentence: "Important to document eyewitness accounts, especially from the 1969 event as people who lived through this event are aging." We sort of chuck-led at this conclusion, even though it was talking about us.

David Brinkley, NBC News, covered the story for two minutes on August 7. Summary—"Tornadoes hit north Minnesota. Approximately 8 tornadoes hit the area. 12 killed, mostly camps and resorts hit. Rescue and search operations continue. Red Cross sets up headquarters. Reporter: Keith Klein, KSTP-TV narrates." Vanderbilt Television News Archive

Walter Cronkite, CBS Evening News, covered the story for about three minutes on August 7. Summary—"Tornadoes kill 13 in northern Minnesota (Outing, Minnesota) 100s of lakeshore homes destroyed or damaged in resort area. 100s injured. (Rescue diver Phil Halper—is looking for bodies.) Copters scour the area, as do National Guard. One couple ducks into their basement shelter and watches roof blow away. Reporter: Joe Bartlemy WCCO-TV." Vanderbilt Television News Archive

Outing Area Tornado Voted Top State Story (in 1969). Minneapolis (AP) "Hardest hit in the August 6 twisters was the Outing area, about 150 miles north of the Twin Cities, where 12 persons died. The storms claimed three more lives while cutting a 140-mile path of death and destruction to the northeast. Although it was the fourth time in five years that killer tornadoes hit the state, the death toll was the highest in 50 years."

Kensie Olson (my 9 year old granddaughter) She typed her own email to me. This brought me to both laughter and tears. My 13 grandchildren strongly motivated me to write the story.

"I remember when I was younger seeing tornado warnings on the news. When I got older (6,7) I thought to my self has any one been in a tornado before in my family? A few years later my

Mimi (sue moline) told me about the outing tornado. She told me she was in that tornado. So I began to gain interest on what happened to my Mimi (sue moline) and other people. Like did my great uncles survive? My great Aunts? While later my Mimi (sue moline) told me not every one survived. My great aunt Becky drowned in Lake Roosevelt. My Mimi's (sue moline) cousin got trapped under a tree at the bottom of the lake and drowned. I felt really bad for her. But throw all of that that made her a tougher person. I know a lot of people have there story's so my Mimi (sue moline) still try's to investigate this tragic story. She has been on Wcco channel 4. It seemed catastrophic the way she told it on the news. I would love to meet all the survivors of that huge tornado. And I know the people who died in the tornado are in heaven having the time of her life. My Bapa (scott moline) married the right woman. She has told are family about this and I am so happy that she is my Mimi. She has told sad stories and happy stories but this one has been saddest one yet. And I know she misses the people she lost. But she has 13 grandchildren and four married daughters and I'm one of grandchildren who has been told the story and we will remember are relatives who has passed and I am Kensie Olson fourth oldest grandchild I have also found old pictures of my great aunt and other people who have past during that sad time. Like my great aunt Becky, my Mimi's (sue moline) cousin Sharon. So when someone mentions the Outing tornado I'll remember my relatives that sadly pasted, and I will see them in heaven when I am there to."

List of Victims and Survivors

Those Who Died in the Outing Tornado (listed youngest to oldest)

Susan Marko—age 2

Sharon Dugan—age 5

Paul Brokke—age 13

Rebecca "Becky" Dugan—age 19

Evelyn "Evy" Carlson—age 50

Rae Knighton—age 54

Edith Dugan—age 62

Olga Long—age 69

Harry Long—age 76

Minnie Olson—age 79

Rev. Arthur Olson—age 80

Jens Gottlieb—age 87

Survivors at the Bethany Cabins (by family)*

Harold Carlson

    Darrell Carlson

    Dale Carlson

Rev. Harold Brokke

    Cathy Brokke

    Daniel Brokke

Rev. LeRoy "Toby" Dugan

    LaVonne "Vonnie" Dugan

    Suzanne (Dugan) Moline

    Lon Dugan

    Jon Dugan

Kenneth Dugan

    Barbara Dugan

    Ronald Dugan

    Donald Dugan

Rev. Richard "Dick" Dugan

    Priscilla Dugan

    Sheila (Dugan) Jensen

    Shane Dugan

    Sheri Dugan (in utero)

Diane (Dugan) Dahlen

Terry Dugan

* I recognize that there were many, many other survivors in this horrific storm along its 38-mile path.

The National Weather Service

For more information: Weather.gov—Search "1969 Outing Tornado" or "Northwoods Tornado Outbreak"

Cass County Clippings, July 2019 (Cass County Historical Society newsletter)—The National Weather Service refers to these storms as the Northwoods Tornado Outbreak. That day, August 6th, at 1:15 p.m. Beltrami County reported the first tornado, a weak F-0, near Bemidji that caused no significant damage. The first damaging tornado, an F-3, touched down west of Backus in the Foot Hills State Forest near Backus at 4:20 p.m. that same day.

| PLACE | DATE | TIME + LOCAL STANDARD | LENGTH OF PATH (MILES) | WIDTH OF PATH (YARDS) | NO. OF PERSONS | | ESTIMATED† DAMAGE | | CHARACTER OF STORM |
					KILLED	INJURED	PROPERTY	CROPS	
Minnesota (continued)									
Cass & Aitken Counties	6	3:48pm 4:28pm	33	¼ to 1½ mi.	12	70	6	0	Tornado

Outing tornado moved between E and ENE at about 50 mph touched down east side of Stewart Lake and moved through the Outing area about 4:00pm and lifted just south of Hill City. On the north side of Outing 2 persons were killed on the west side of Roosevelt Lake, 9 were killed on the east side, and one person near Reservoir Lake. Damage to property, utilities and stumpage $2,150,000. The tree damage showed circular winds on the ground with varying widths. Over Outing the tornado was nearly 1½ miles wide. The general pattern was similar to the Floodwood tornado.

CST

The first killer tornado that was an F-4 touched down near Stewart Lake in northwestern Crow Wing County at 4:48 p.m. The tornado traveled northeast more than 30 miles across southeastern Cass County to just south of Hill City in Aitkin County. Between 5 and 7 p.m., as many as nine more F-2 and F-3 tornadoes touched down near Chisholm, Jacobson, Tower-Soudan, Ely, Floodwood and Two Harbors. Twelve people died as a result of the Outing tornado and 74 people were injured with 70 of those having serious injuries. The Outing tornado had the longest path of 32.3 miles*

and the widest path of 833 yards and was the deadliest tornado outbreak in the recorded history of northern Minnesota.

* *The NWS later revised the tornado path to 38 miles.*

Meeting with the National Weather Service, Duluth, Minnesota June 12, 2019, Terry, NWS meteorologist Joseph Moore, Sue, Diane, NWS meteorologist Dan Miller

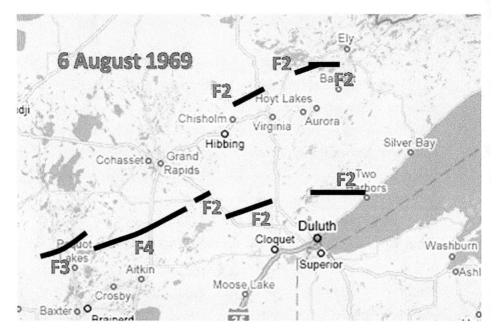

Locations and intensity of all the tornados in the Northwoods tornado outbreak of August 6, 1969

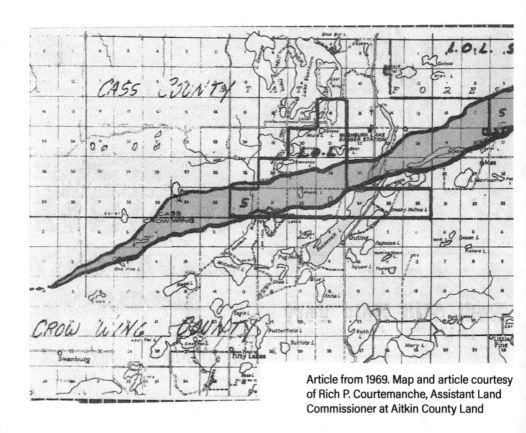

Article from 1969. Map and article courtesy of Rich P. Courtemanche, Assistant Land Commissioner at Aitkin County Land

Sue studying weather history maps at the NWS offices in Duluth.

The forestry map below shows the entire path of the Outing tornado. The damage was surveyed three times.

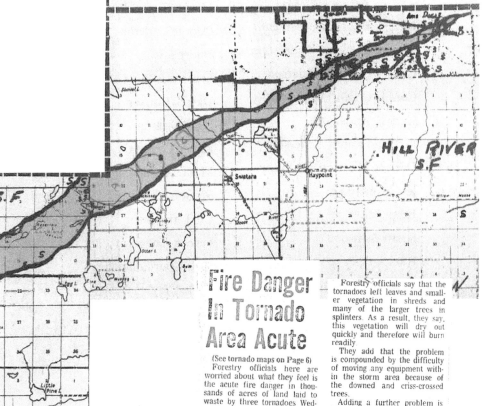

Fire Danger In Tornado Area Acute

(See tornado maps on Page 6)

Forestry officials here are worried about what they feel is the acute fire danger in thousands of acres of land laid to waste by three tornadoes Wednesday, August 6.

James E. Spangler, regional forester, said it is estimated that there is a total of 54 sections or 34,560 acres of blowdown in the paths of the three twisters with 12 sections or 7,680 acres being on state land.

Spangler estimated the value of the timber on the state land along at $50,000.

The paths of the three tornadoes were plotted on maps after Bill Morris, game warden, and Cliff Carlson, assistant regional forester, made extensive flights over the area.

Forestry officials say that the tornadoes left leaves and smaller vegetation in shreds and many of the larger trees in splinters. As a result, they say, this vegetation will dry out quickly and therefore will burn readily.

They add that the problem is compounded by the difficulty of moving any equipment within the storm area because of the downed and criss-crossed trees.

Adding a further problem is the lack of rainfall.

It was pointed out that burning will be permitted in designated areas only or by special permit issued by the local district forester.

In an effort to solve the problem, the forestry department has hired a tractor operator to make an attempt at bunching the downed timber and cutting firebreaks.

Spangler said that the blow-

TORNADO
Continued on Page 2

Eyewitnesses and Contributors

Greg Achterling

Joe Aiello

Tim Andersen—*Cass County Historical Society & Museum*

Bruce and Wendi Andersohn

Connie (Busby) Anderson

Connie (Malm) Anderson

Gary E. Anderson

Rick and Karen Anderson

Darlene (Carlson) Anthony

Joe Armstrong

Betsy Asher

Susan Ashwood

Patrick Baier

NaDeen Barnum

Terry Berczyk

Bill Berg

Terry Berg

Van Bialon

Paul Boblett—*Northland Press*

Ronald Bode

Carol (Ashcraft) Bordwell

Marlies Brinkman

Catherine Brokke

Daniel Brokke

Rodney Buckingham

Marge (Zagar) Burns

George Carleton

Dale Carlson

Dan Carlson

Darrell Carlson

Dave Carlson

Nancy Carlson

Mark Cermak

Vernon Chenevert

Civil Air Patrol

Patrick Coughlin

Rich Courtemanche

Carla Cray

Randy Cray

Patricia Czyson

Diane (Dugan) Dahlen

Martha Davidge

Mary Jane Derscheid

Bill Donnelly

James Dowson

Barbara Dugan

Don Dugan

Jon Dugan

Lon Dugan

Ron Dugan

Patrick Dugan

Priscilla Dugan

Shane Dugan

Terry Dugan

Sue Duncan

Joan Edlund

Steve Eliason

Kathie Esser

Erik Evenson

Linda Evenson

Jerry Ferguson

Jim Filkins

Matt Gaines

Margaret Genung

Renee Geving—*Cass County Historical Society & Museum*

Patti (Muck) Giese

Aaron Goodyear—WCCO TV

Barb Grove

Fred and Lynda Hall

Phil Halper—*Minnesota Para Rescue Team*

Mike Hanks

Matt Hanson

Mary (Zier) Havenor

Alice (Olds) Hawkinson

Nancy (Borris) Holscher

Annette Houg

Jim Hunt

Jeremy S. Jackson

Robert Jarvi

Sheila (Dugan) Jensen

Alan Johnson

Brooks Johnson

Carol and Gary Johnson

Shirley Johnson

Ruthie Kauffman

Bob Kleinschmidt

Anne Kletten

Carol (Zagar) Korte

Pam (Roach) Kuschel

Lori LaBorde

Denny Lee

Ellen Leger

Curtis Letch

Candace Lilyquist

Mery Lysne

Patrick Maranda

Jeanna Marko

Pamela Marko

Bill Matthies & Gary Fitch—*divers*

Jim Matthies

Jennifer Mayerle—*WCCO TV*

Jean (Simmons) McKeever

Cecelia McKeig

Pat Meyer

Cindy Miller

Dan Miller—*National Weather Service (Duluth)*

Pete Mohs—*The Brainerd Dispatch*

Joseph Moore—*National Weather Service (Duluth)*

Roberta Munck

Charles Nelson

Robert Norman

Glenda Fawkes Nyberg

Alan Arthur Olson

Chad Olson

Diana Olson

Tim Olson

David Peppin

Sandra Plifka

Denise (Gibis) Ramacier

Dennis and Julie Recknor

Nancy Reich

Ron Reich

Tom Riedesel

Dr. Jean Rock

Lynn Rogers

Deborah Rose—*Mn Department of Natural Resources*

Andy Ruigh

David Rykken

Sue Schaefer

Dave Schaumburg

Bruce Schindler

Andrew Scott

Shirley Shaw

Eddy Silker

Alice "Teddy" Skattum

Phil Slinden

Rev. and Mrs. Jim Slye

Terry Slye

Belinda Stealy

Chris Steiner

Dan Steiner

Darla Mae Swanson

Tim Taylor

Dennis Tennison

Diana Thomas

Elsie Tollgaard

Nancy VanVorst-Toth

Mike Turner

Tammy Wall

Rick Wigand

Kay Wittgenstein

Florence Wodarz

Blake Wolney

Patricia (Rotar) Youker

Kathryn Runman-Zimney

Sue Dugan Moline

Sue Moline is a survivor of the Outing tornado that took the lives of her sister, grandmother and cousin and shares with us in this personal drama and tragedy a memory that refuses to be silenced. As the 50th anniversary of this infamous day approached, Sue felt an urgency to find the "missing" pieces to this story that had haunted her for decades and launched her into a personal mission of discovery. This moving book is a result of that research.

She is a graduate of Bethany Global University, and in 1985 started her own successful business, Words to Go, Inc.

A devoted wife to her high school sweetheart, Scott, together they have four grown daughters and 13 grandchildren and reside in Bloomington, Minnesota. Sue enjoys reading, gardening, weekends at the lake, and her grandchildren's activities in her spare time.

*To purchase additional copies visit
Amazon.com, or duganbooks.com*

*For additional information
or to contact the author, go to
thelaketurnedupsidedown.com*

Printed in the USA
CPSIA information can be obtained
at www.ICGtesting.com
LVHW022215181123
764337LV00012B/795